Christian Classics Revisited

Christian Classics Revisited

BY

JAMES J. THOMPSON, JR.

BR
117
.T48
1983

IGNATIUS PRESS   SAN FRANCISCO

Cover by Victoria Hoke

With ecclesiastical approval
© 1983 by Ignatius Press
All rights reserved
ISBN 0–89870–028–0
Library of Congress Catalogue number 82–84583
Printed in the United States of America

TO

NANCY

TABLE OF CONTENTS

FOREWORD

It was a delight to be asked to write the Foreword to this book of essays, especially because it is a vindication of sorts—and I'm still spiritually frail enough to crave public vindication. You see, I regard James J. Thompson, Jr., as one of the hottest literary talents around—and I insist that, as Editor of the *New Oxford Review*, I discovered him. I want this fact recorded for posterity—even if the Lord gives me my comeuppance on Judgment Day (see Luke 14:11).

To be entirely serious: Jim Thompson is a remarkable thinker and writer, the kind whose writing is so polished, whose logic so finely tuned, and whose depth of learning and intuition so profound that he intimidates editors. I mean, if everyone started writing as he does, editors would become functionally superfluous—relegated, one by one, to this nation's already crowded soup kitchens and unemployment lines.

Although Jim is still relatively young and unknown, I'm confident he is going to leave his mark on the history of American letters. This book you are about to read is not, however, a vain exercise in "art for art's sake". These essays have a *message*—and one that springs from one man's strenuous walk with the Lord. The purpose of the essays collected here—which were inaugurated in the November 1979 *New Oxford Review* and will, I hope, continue indefinitely—is to prevent the more recent classics of Christian literature from slipping into obscurity, and—even more importantly—to remind believers that these classics have the power to enhance our spiritual lives.

But, in an uncanny way, Jim's essays are more than guides and pointers and reminders (though they are all these). His essays are so spiritually rich that they themselves have the power to bless you—at least I have found that to be so in my own life.

I thank God for Jim Thompson—and for somehow having sent Jim my way. And yes, *to the Lord*—not to me and not even to Jim—be all the glory.

DALE VREE
Berkeley, California
September 1982

PREFACE

Can a book—other than the Bible, of course—save one's soul? The definitive answer to that question must await that moment when each individual stands before the Seat of Judgment. In the meantime, we toil along a narrow and twisting road, seeking truth wherever it may be found and hoping passionately that God will shower his mercy upon us.

The essays in this volume operate on the premise that books—specifically the testimonies of Christian writers (whether cast as novels, autobiographies, biographies, theological treatises or meditations)—can facilitate the pilgrim's journey through life and can even be the means through which God imparts saving grace to undeserving sinners. The works of Graham Greene and Georges Bernanos illuminate the dark caverns of despair and enable those who have lost hope to place their own plight within the grand scheme of salvation. John Woolman and Dorothy Day remind one that the true Christian must plunge into the ruck and moil of temporal suffering, must sacrifice all for the "least of these" whom God loves most.

Evelyn Waugh and T. S. Eliot force one to confront the frightening fact that life itself must sometimes be forsaken to follow God. Here in these writers is truth, vital pulsating truth that can change one's life, can pierce through that hard carapace of sin and puncture the mundaneness and complacency of existence. If these essays help to lead even one person to such an experience, then I shall have succeeded beyond my wildest imaginings.

Another motive underlies these essays: my need to explore the ramifications of my own belief and to resolve some of the questions that have arisen out of my own experience. I wish I could claim that these twenty-five books have banished all the doubts and answered all the questions; unfortunately I cannot. One thing has become clear, though: spiritual guidance comes in many guises and truth springs from many quarters. The Catholics, Anglicans, Baptists, Quakers and Reformed Christians who appear in these pages all contribute their part toward answering those most momentous of questions: What does it mean to be a Christian? What must one do to be saved? For some, the answers come through the tortuous way of anguish; for others, through the self-sacrifice of service to one's fellow man. Some look to an intellection that rallies reason to God's cause, while others abide in a childlike faith in the promises of Jesus Christ. To borrow a phrase from William James, these writers exemplify "the varieties of religious experience"; I do not believe that one can afford to ignore any of them in his efforts to be a Christian.

It would be deeply satisfying to say that these books have made me a better Christian; that would be prideful, however, for only God can make that judgment. At the least, though, they have enabled me to understand better what it means to call oneself a follower of Christ. They have shown the way; it is up to me—and to everyone—to set forth on the journey.

I scarcely know how to thank Dale Vree, editor of the *New Oxford Review*, for all he has done for me. Without him this book would not exist. Three years ago he opened the pages of his magazine to me, an unknown writer who from his slim record of publication hardly had the right to call himself a writer. Throughout our association since then he has encouraged, prodded and criticized, each in perfect measure and each at the precise time when it was needed. He convinced me that these essays deserved to be turned into a book, and he magnanimously permitted me to use the materials originally printed (in altered form) in the *New Oxford Review* between November 1979 and October 1982. But Dale Vree is more than an inspiring editor; he is a follower of Christ who—as much as any writer discussed in this book—has shown me what it means to be a Christian.

Others have made this book possible as well. The readers of the *New Oxford Review* have heartened me with their continued interest in my reflections on Christian writers. In letters both to me and to the magazine they have convinced me that my labors have been richly rewarded. I owe a special debt to Father Joseph Fessio, S.J., editor of Ignatius Press, for his willingness to undertake that always risky venture of transforming a manuscript into á book. I also wish to thank the production staff of Ignatius Press for the careful attention given to my manuscript.

Finally, I thank my wife, Nancy, to whom this book is dedicated. To depart from the usual tribute: she did not edit my prose, nor did she type the manuscript, nor did she keep the children quiet while I wrote (we haven't any anyway). She did, however, give me what a writer needs most of all: faith in myself and the determination to persist in my work. To say that this book is hers too would be to understate my indebtedness to her.

JAMES J. THOMPSON, JR.
Nashville, Tennessee
November 1982

I

GRAHAM GREENE'S

The Power and the Glory

A favorite bumper sticker of born-again Christians invites one to "Smile—Jesus Loves You", while another proclaims "I Found It!" College students punctuate their conversations with exclamations of "Praise the Lord!" Young charismatics testify to their regular and direct communication with God, a deity who answers their prayers and guides them over the shoals of life. No subtlety here; the message is clear: cast yourself upon Jesus Christ, shed your cares and sorrows and discover rest and comfort in the arms of the Savior. Who in this world of nameless (and nameable) terror and gnawing fear could resist such an invitation?

Not all who answer that call find the peace that passeth understanding. The attempt to believe traps some in the despair of souls who cry out to God and hear only the echoes of their own plaintive pleas. In the twentieth century few have laid bare the torments of such souls with more perspicacity and compassion than the English novelist and Roman Catholic convert Graham Greene. Although he has illuminated the conflict that rages in the same heart between belief and unbelief in such powerful novels as *The End of the Affair* and *The Heart of the Matter*, Greene presented his most compelling treatment of this theme in *The Power and the Glory*, a work published some forty years ago.

Greene unfolds his drama of spiritual struggle on the stage of a backward, dismally poor region of Mexico in the early 1930s. Within the maelstrom of revolutionary chaos that gripped Mexico in the first decades of the twentieth century this small state has razed the churches and murdered the priests. In its quest to establish a new order cleansed of the hunger and want of the priest-ridden society of old, the revolutionary government intends to erase every trace of Roman Catholicism: "One day they'll forget there ever was a Church here." Only two priests remain: Padre José, who, to save his life, has gone meekly to the marriage bed with his former housekeeper, and an unnamed priest—the protagonist of the novel—who steals from village to village, hearing confessions and bringing the Body and Blood of Christ to the peons. How easily, in less subtle hands, these raw materials might have been turned into a one-dimensional tale of physical courage and spiritual intrepidity, a morality play in which unsullied Good bests the Forces of Evil. Greene possesses instead a more complex vision of the workings of grace and of how one ascends to holiness. His priest, an unprepossessing little man with "protuberant eyes" and "death . . . in his carious mouth", is a drunkard who has fathered a child and who cries out unheroically: "Let me be caught soon. . . . Let me be caught." The demands of his vocation permit him no rest; the easy way of renunciation lies closed to him. He wears his faith like a "birthmark".

Against this priest Greene pits a police lieutenant in whose heart burn the implacable hatred and devouring love of one sworn to destroy priestcraft and to purge his land of injustice and superstition. "There was something of a priest in his intent observant walk—a theologian going back over the errors of the past to destroy them again." He annunciates a new truth to replace the outmoded message of a merciful God who paid the supreme price for sinners: he bears the gospel of "a vacant universe and a cooling world" where men make their own happiness, free from the baleful eye of God. Nothing will prevent the lieutenant from seizing his prey; he will, if need be, scourge the land—murdering and terrorizing the peons whom he loves—to bring his quarry to bay. No price is too great to pay in order to translate into reality his dream of a perfect social order.

The priest offers the ragged villagers no such promise of temporal salvation; he, a "bad priest", can only place the Body of Christ upon their tongues and with the words *Hoc est enim Corpus Meum* illumine the darkness of their lives with a piercing shaft of light. He harbors no hope for himself. In a moment of drunken despair seven years ago he had lurched into the arms of a woman; from that unholy union had come a daughter, born of sin but still a child of God. Penitence will not come to the priest, for he fiercely loves this daughter with a passion he had been incapable of in the prideful innocence of his youth. His wrong-doing has enabled him to love. He absolves others, even those guilty of the seductive sins of complacency and false piety, but his own words of contrition die upon his lips.

Given the opportunity to escape across the mountains to safety in a neighboring state, the priest instead turns back to offer absolution to a dying murderer and to fall knowingly into a trap set by the police lieutenant. To his betrayer, a degenerate, whining mestizo, he says: "I'll pray for you." Without protest he follows the lieutenant back to accept the release from anguish promised by the bullets of a firing squad. Touched deeply—if only briefly—by this strange priest, the lieutenant tries to persuade Padre José to hear the condemned man's last confession; when his entreaties fail, the lieutenant offers his captive a final solace: a bottle of brandy, which the priest drinks during the long night before his execution. The priest goes to his death thinking not of his own damnation nor of the moment of pain; "he felt only an immense disappointment because he had to go to God empty-handed, with nothing done at all. . . . He knew now that at the end there was only one thing that counted—to be a saint."

The spiritual torment of Greene's Mexican priest will seem odd to those who happen upon *The Power and the Glory* in this age of situation ethics, an era presided over by an enlightened God who smiles benevolently upon man's antics. After the "Me Decade" of the 1970s, with its psychological gimmicks guaranteed to make everyone realize that "I'm okay", this sad man appears in a poor light. What he needs is plain to anyone: renewed self-esteem and a God who encourages priests to express themselves sexually. Proponents of liberation theology have a different solution to the priest's problems: he could have avoided all that useless soul-searching by leaguing with the police lieutenant to usher in a new day for the oppressed peons. Why not follow the example of the guerrilla clerics of Latin America? Greene's hapless priest is too old-fashioned to appeal to today's Christians.

Is he? At the risk of being labeled hopelessly reactionary one may hazard a different view. The odyssey of the agonizing soul threading its way to the Throne of Glory will never lose its poignant currency for those Christians—however small their number may become—who believe that eternal salvation remains man's ultimate goal. There will always be those like Greene's priest for whom the lacerated wounds of sin will not be easily healed. The ways of God remain veiled to our feeble eyes, but the wonderful mystery of his grace has performed stranger feats than to save the soul of a whisky priest guilty of fornication or (Dare one suggest?) to elevate him to sainthood. To be a saint—that is indeed what counts.

II

G. K. Chesterton's

Orthodoxy

A disturbing contradiction besets American society: on every side one beholds the celebrators of life, those terribly sincere and well-meaning men and women who bemoan the plight of snail darters and baby seals. At the same time, many of these self-proclaimed kinsmen of all living creatures rally to the abortion movement. What is one to do with such a massive perversion of the Christian imperative to love and to cherish the fruits of God's creation? I too like whales, but the temptation to festoon the trees in my front yard with banners urging "Nuke the Whales" almost overwhelms me at times. Resisting that temptation reluctantly, I turn instead to G. K. Chesterton's *Orthodoxy*, there to find, not John Denver's treacly banalities about Rocky Mountain highs, but a truly Christian love of nature as "a little dancing sister, to be laughed at as well as loved".

That a book published in 1908 should serve to combat the idiocies of the 1980s may appear strange at first, but who better to fathom the nature of vicious silliness than one who reached maturity in the England of Beatrice and Sidney Webb, those twin monuments to man's time-honored capacity for making a fool (note: not a Holy Fool) of himself? In his ability to speak to our age Chesterton belongs with two other Englishmen of this century: Hilaire Belloc and C. S. Lewis. As members of what might be called the "pipe and pint" school of Christian apologetics, these men fought fiercely for the eternal verities of Christianity, while fully appreciating that, as Chesterton remarked, "life is not only a pleasure but a kind of eccentric privilege." They appeal to those Christians who long for union with Christ in heaven yet who savor the joys of the moment—symbolized by the pint of ale and the pipeful of tobacco—as they move toward the Seat of Judgment. Lewis enjoys preeminence among this trio, but Chesterton—with at least four books of supreme excellence to his credit: *The Everlasting Man*, *St. Francis of Assisi*, *St. Thomas Aquinas* and *Orthodoxy* (Chestertonians will rightly insist on expanding this list)—need take no backseat to C. S. Lewis.

One can scarcely imagine a Christian not taking to Chesterton; how could one resist the spiritual vigor that permeates *Orthodoxy*? Yet there are some who disdain him. Taking for granted that religious liberals find him too conservative for their tastes, one must acknowledge another group of Christians who elude the Chestertonian spell: those whose search for God entangles them in the web of despair. In his book *The Varieties of Religious Experience* William James typed these believers as "sick souls"; oppressed by the preponderance of evil, they often succumb to the bleakest of pessimism. Chesterton by contrast partook heavily of what James called the "religion of the healthy-minded". These fortunate folk revel in the goodness of creation; filled with high spirits and good cheer, they stride through life at peace with themselves and their Creator.

With scarcely a glance toward the abyss Chesterton presents in *Orthodoxy* the account of how one rotund Englishman (himself) marched resolutely forth from the citadel of adolescent agnosticism to arrive at the startling conclusion that Christians had been right all along. "I freely confess all the idiotic ambitions of the end of the nineteenth century", he writes. "I did, like all other solemn little boys, try to be in advance of the truth. And I found that I was eighteen hundred years behind it."

To follow step by step Chesterton's journey to discovery would take too long in a short essay and would, moreover, deprive the prospective reader of the pleasure of having Chesterton himself lead one in his footsteps. Two chapters—"The Flag of the World" and "The Paradoxes of Christianity" —suffice to illustrate how Chesterton uncovered the solutions to his "own solitary and sincere speculations". In these chapters he recounts how Christianity illuminated and then transformed two characteristic features of his intellectual landscape: his resolute optimism and his delight in paradox.

Christianity taught Chesterton that true optimism lifts one's eyes beyond this world to gaze steadily upon the promise of eternal life. This elevated perspective does not permit one to despise the temporal: because we love God's creation —and harbor hope for it—we strive to make it better; it is ours, if only for a season. The cares, the toils, the sorrows of this earth need not dishearten us, for we belong ultimately to another country, the Kingdom of God.

The marvellous paradoxes of the Christian experience enthralled Chesterton. In Christianity he discovered a faith for all men, for unlike the Golden Mean of the Greek philosophers it does not draw everything toward a middle way; instead, the Church embraces—even encourages—the clash of violent extremes and seeks no synthesizing resolution of these opposites. The warrior and the peacemaker, the monk and the statesman, the pessimist and the optimist—all find a home within the Body of Christ. Christianity preserves these "furious opposites, by keeping them both, and keeping them both furious".

In every age God chooses and anoints his champions; in the depths of secularity there will always be those who bear God's truth unflinchingly. G. K. Chesterton bore it in his age. If anything, God's cause is more beleaguered today than in Chesterton's time, but the cause is just and right and it *will* triumph. In the grimmest of times Chesterton can recall one to that essential fact.

Were I so bold as to peer into that which is shut off from mortal eyes, I might envisage G. K. Chesterton enjoying the heavenly rewards of his labor. There he sits in all his robust splendor, brandy glass in one hand, cigar in the other, regaling his auditors with tales of his clashes with George Bernard Shaw and other votaries of the modern creed. Irreverent? If so, perhaps our vision of heaven suffers from a certain bloodlessness. I do not think my suggestion would discomfit one who could end *Orthodoxy* with these words: "There was some one thing that was too great for God to show us when he walked upon our earth; and I have sometimes fancied that it was his mirth." If we do indeed have a God of mirth he found his perfect paladin in a large, exuberant Englishman named Gilbert Keith Chesterton.

III

GEORGES BERNANOS'

The Diary of a Country Priest

"Georges Bernanos? Never heard of him." How many times have I gritted my teeth at that refrain as I have tried with a nagging persistence to convince my friends to read this disturbing Frenchman who by turns infuriated and intrigued his countrymen from the 1920s through the 1940s? One needs no Gallup poll to prove that Bernanos commands at best only a small following in the United States. While Proust, Gide, Sartre and Camus continue to be read avidly and to have their ideas bruited about with enthusiasm, Bernanos' books pine away in university libraries, patiently waiting to be perused by other than a stray scholar or two. Perhaps Bernanos expounded too many alien ideas to appeal to an American audience. How many Americans will attempt to fathom the mind of an intensely devout—yet anti-clerical—Roman Catholic monarchist who despised the very things Americans treasure: bourgeois democracy, capitalism, material comfort and an abiding faith in the ability of vigor, energy and talent to solve life's problems? Those willing to give Bernanos a chance might begin with his masterpiece, *The Diary of a Country Priest*, a novel published in France in 1936.

To call this book a novel in the popular sense may be misleading, for as the title indicates, Bernanos constructs the story through diary entries made over a brief period by an obscure young priest of the parish of Ambricourt in the region of Artois. Little actually happens: the nameless priest pursues his debilitating and numbing ministry to his peasant parishioners while flagellating himself with self-doubt and despair. The villagers view him as an ineffectual and bumbling fool; contempt and pity mingle in their eyes as they watch him fail miserably in his attempts to revivify the Word of God among them.

The book's dynamic arises from the tensions of the priest's inner life as revealed in the agony that he daily notes in the pages of his diary. He knows his own inadequacies better than do the villagers; he sees clearly that his love for them and his compassion for their suffering appear as "a kind of ridiculous embarrassment that must make people feel very uncomfortable". Even worse, he must wrestle with despair as he stands mute before God, unable to discern the workings of grace either among his parishioners or in his own heart. He chafes under his clerical superiors: desk bishops who care only for well-organized parishes and dutiful priests; spiritually complacent churchmen who mouth platitudes while the people drown in boredom; sophisticated clerics who cultivate cleverness to gain entrée to fashionable salons; and cowardly, well-fed curates who truckle to the rich and powerful.

Faced with an overwhelming sense of his failure, the young priest turns to the Curé de Torcy, a tough, wise old priest from a neighboring parish. The Curé refuses to grant his colleague the meretricious comforts of pity. He flings the priest's complaints back in his face, chides him for his weakness and braces him with the counsel of experience. With a peasant bluntness the Curé explicates the nature of truth, the role of the Church and her priests, the implacability of man's sinfulness, the meaning of poverty and the way of prayer. He reminds his colleague that "a parish is bound to be dirty. A whole Christian society's a lot dirtier. You wait for the Judgment Day and see what the angels'll be sweeping out of even the most saintly monasteries. Some filth!" The world cannot be shaped to an ideal; its imperfections render it "rather like old man Job, stretched out in all his filth, covered with ulcers and sores". To this world of sinful men God's servants bring the "red-hot iron" of truth and the will to discipline, to restore order, ever mindful that "night is bound to turn the day's work upside down—night belongs to the devil." The Curé impresses two facts upon his friend: the Church carries joy to a human race steeped in sadness and weariness; and, though the Church bears the gift of gladness, God calls some men to a vocation of suffering. The young priest finally realizes "that I am never to be torn from that eternal place chosen for me—that I remain the prisoner of his Agony in the Garden."

This man of agony suffers not only in spirit: his body harbors, as he belatedly discovers, a savage cancer that has dragged him to the edge of death. As death beckons, the priest stares unflinchingly into its face and—in the last pages of his diary— makes his peace with God and with himself. The anguish, the self-doubt, the frustration of his ministry fade as he understands that his very agony has been "beyond all an act of love" offered to God. Now reconciled to himself, to the "poor, poor shell of me", he perceives that "the supreme grace would be to love oneself in all simplicity—as one would love any one of those who themselves have suffered and loved in Christ." As the priest dies, a friend—himself a former priest—bends his ear to the dying man's lips and hears his last faint words: "Does it matter? Grace is everywhere. . . ."

The Diary of a Country Priest unveils to often unreceptive eyes a painful but vital truth: saints do not always come cloaked in easily recognizable garb. The saintliness of a Mother Teresa of Calcutta, stooping to bathe the suppurating sores of a dying beggar, moves the hearts of even the most cynical of men. Bernanos refuses one the comforts of such an obvious and unambiguous example of the power of God's love and grace. He confronts one with the saint as a figure of torment and self-doubt, reviled by his fellow men and forced to suffer the torture of apparent alienation from God. Bernanos renders graphically a stunning paradox: he who strikes his fellow men as feckless and inconsequential may stand before God wreathed in the ineffable majesty of divine love. Jesus Christ must have cut a poor figure among his contemporaries. The rich, the well-born, the powerful and those of all stations whose hearts had become encrusted with the grime of sin easily scorned this lowly Jew who bore without protest the degradations heaped upon him, even to the final disgrace of crucifixion on a rude cross. Just so, Bernanos' obscure priest loves with a deep and consuming passion, but in return he receives only contempt, pity and mockery. To modern secular man Bernanos' protagonist must present a perplexing study. But for the believer in Christ's redemptive death, Bernanos has limned with a deft touch a portrait of self-sacrifice and suffering. Truly, grace *is* everywhere.

IV

ROMANO GUARDINI'S

The Lord

First the bad news: this hefty volume runs to 535 pages and it comes from the hand of a learned theologian, one of the deepest Catholic thinkers of the twentieth century. Dare I urge it upon you, knowing full well that you have already decided to forgo the dubious pleasure of venturing into a thicket of impenetrable prose and recondite theology? Without apology, yes, for the good news will quickly dispel the dread you have conjured up: Monsignor Guardini, the Italian-German author of *The Lord* (first published in the United States in 1954), paints with a bold and sure hand a portrait of Jesus Christ that every Christian must behold for himself.

The Lord has not always fared well at the hands of his biographers. Since the nineteenth century a succession of rationalist detractors has stripped Christ of his divinity, reduced him to the merely human and left orthodox Christians gasping at such blasphemous arrogance. The defenders of

Jesus Christ have often served him as poorly, for they have frequently fabricated a saccharine Christ who strolled the Holy Land smiling wanly and exuding a squeaky-clean goodness. Both views leave one searching in vain for that powerful and holy figure who came to this earth to redeem fallen man from sin.

Monsignor Guardini recognizes the perils of his undertaking. He cautions at the outset that one cannot fathom the inner workings of Christ's mind, nor can one pursue confidently the biographer's usual task of setting the historical stage, tracing the pertinent influences and emerging with a skillfully drawn account of the evolution of a life. No, says Guardini, for at the core of Christ's person dwells the *"mysterium Dei*, canceler of all psychology"*, who "came to us out of the fullness of time contained in the mystery of God."

Although Guardini writes from a background of vast learning and lifelong immersion in scholarship, he ventures no ponderous exegeses or dazzling displays of erudition. He offers instead the simple fruits of "some four years of Sunday services undertaken with the sole purpose of obeying as well as possible the Lord's command to proclaim him, his message and works." From Matthew to Revelation, from the Virgin Birth to the fearsome events that will swirl about the Second Coming, Guardini accomplishes just that.

Ranging across the entire New Testament he
unfolds the life of Christ and reveals the Christian
message embedded in the New Testament canon.

One could easily fill many pages in detailing
the immense breadth of Guardini's sweeping
commentary on Christ's life. Hardly a topic remains untouched and those touched are illumined.
Guardini's treatment of two perennially vexatious
subjects provides a sample of the wisdom and
insight that emerge from the pages of *The Lord*.

Even a cursory glance at the teachings of Jesus
Christ reveals a recurring theme: man exists in a
world of fellow men to whom he owes considerable obligation. The Christian cannot shut himself
off from his fellows and in isolated obliviousness
pursue the salvation of his soul. Christianity en-
tails a social ethic and from that commitment
arises the troublesome problem of the Christian's
specific duties to those around him. Guardini faces
this matter squarely, refusing to sidestep it dex-
terously with a few glib pieties. He forces one to
confront an essential fact of the Christian message:
"It is impossible to love God without loving your
neighbor. Love is a stream that flows from God to
me, from me to my neighbor (and not to one only,
but to all), from my neighbor back to God. This is
no longer individualism, but vital communalism."
Some Christians use this as a justification to fash-
ion Christ into an earthly reformer who embodies

the hope and promise of a just and love-filled temporal order. With a Christ such as this, then, the Christian has no choice but to pledge his allegiance to every movement that purports to eradicate injustice. From this logic spring the guerrilla priests of Latin America and the clerical theorists who urge an alliance between Marxism and Christianity. For Guardini such reasoning misleads Christians; it offers only an attenuated gospel of social salvation instead of the fullness of Christ's message.

Make no mistake, though: Guardini will not allow the Christian to excuse himself from the messy realities of want, hatred and the violation of elemental human rights. Christ clearly enjoins his followers to minister to the ills of suffering human beings. Guardini discerns what dedicated architects of a better world often miss: Christ "sees the mystery of suffering much more profoundly— deep at the root-tip of human existence, and inseparable from sin and estrangement from God." Only a compassion rooted in the desire to reconcile man to man and both to God saves one from a misguided—and often bloody—attempt to create a utopia free from suffering. Relief from the "stupidity, injustice, deception and violence" that make of man's existence such a misery "can come only from God, after earthly life is over."

This leads to Guardini's penetrating discussion of the Second Coming of Christ. It distresses him that Christians have become so enmeshed in the mundane that they have lost sight of Christ's promise to return in glory to foreclose on human history. To a world preoccupied with its own paltry activities—however noble and important they may appear to finite man—Guardini brings a reminder that "both we as individuals and the world as a whole live under the ever-present possibility of judgment." He rattles the foundations of complacency when he warns that this earth "is God's property, of which he can dispose as he pleases—even if, in the meantime, it has become 'modern' and ceases to believe in him." This world will end whether or not we give our assent and, as Guardini wisely counsels, we had best pursue our lives with that sobering thought clearly before us. Serve one's fellow man—yes; savor the goodness of God's creation—yes; but keep one's vision trained steadily on that final Day of Judgment.

The orthodox Christian lives today at a time when relentless evil assails him on every side; despair tugs at his heart and clouds his mind with doubt. Guardini understands this, and herein lies the ultimate importance of *The Lord*. This book can guide the Christian through the treacherous byways of the world and, while accomplishing this, it entreats the believer to look forward confidently to that day when Christ will return to mete out divine justice. Then the Lord will pronounce those longed-for words of commendation: "Well done thou good and faithful servants."

V

IGNAZIO SILONE'S

Bread and Wine

Subtlety of characterization is not one of Ignazio Silone's strong points in his novel of 1937, *Bread and Wine*: his attack on Italian Fascism pits unblemished Good against unadulterated Evil. On the side of the angels stand the old priest Don Benedetto, who dies for his "liberty of spirit" and "great humanity", and Pietro Spina, the righteous revolutionary. Arrayed against them are the Forces of Iniquity: Fascist thugs; a rich and flaccid Roman Catholic Church ruled by Pope "Pontius XI"; and a supporting cast of landlords, bankers, tax collectors, militarists, demagogues and lackeys.

Why bother with a novel replete with the stereotypes that prompted many of the leftists of the 1930s to consign their critical faculties to cold storage? *Bread and Wine* has been acclaimed by leftist ideologues and literary opinion makers as a great *anti-Fascist* novel, but not as a Christian classic. One is tempted to dismiss the book as nothing more than a better-than-average contribution to the genre of "socialist realism" that flourished in the '30s under the aegis of the cultural commissars of the Kremlin. There is more to Silone, however; he deserves better than to be relegated to that legion of men and women of slim talents and fat pretensions who subjected art—and morality—to the demands of agitprop. Silone cannot be written off so easily; the moral force of the man and the writer must be reckoned with.

Silone loved Italy passionately, especially his native region of the Abruzzi; out of that deep love, and from his exile in Switzerland, he wrote *Bread and Wine* to voice the anguish of those who suffered the ravages of Fascism under Benito Mussolini (referred to as "Etcetera Etcetera" in the book) and his blackshirted henchmen. By 1937 Silone had long since exited the Communist Party—the Italian branch of which he had helped to found in 1921—having discovered, as he later wrote in his essay in *The God That Failed*, that "the increasing degeneration of the Communist International into a tyranny and a bureaucracy filled me with repulsion and disgust." From the ruins of his Communist faith Silone salvaged a non-Marxist socialism and wedded it to a primitive Christianity that sought to usher in the "ancient hope of the Kingdom of God on earth, the old expectation of charity taking the place of law. . . ."

Out of his own struggle with the regnant fanaticisms of the 1920s and 1930s Silone created Pietro Spina, a seasoned and determined revolutionary who returns to Italy from exile on the eve of the Italian invasion of Ethiopia in 1935. Struck down by a wasting disease in his lungs, Spina must seek a refuge where he can recover his strength and plan his attack on the Fascist overlords of his homeland. Disguised as a recuperating priest from another diocese he settles in the tiny village of Pietrasecca, not far from the town of his boyhood. The return to the scene of his youth, combined with the veneration and respect accorded the visiting "priest" by the villagers, provokes a clash between the lingering traces of Spina's Catholic upbringing and his new religion of Marxism. Revived memories of his schooling under Don Benedetto, a saintly priest who had preached charity and brotherhood to his charges, nags at Spina's commitment to violent revolution.

> Imperceptibly the adolescent who had gone to catechism every evening to prepare for the First Communion was resurrected; the schoolboy who had devoured the lives of the saints and argued with Don Benedetto about ways of living without compromise. Imperceptibly a colloquy started between the revolutionary who had been superimposed upon his adolescent self and the adolescent in him who was not yet dead.

Troubled by this conflict Spina seeks out his old teacher for guidance. Speaking in a voice not of "an atheist, but that of a disappointed lover", Spina insists to his mentor that he has abandoned religion. Soon after his visit with Don Benedetto, though, he realizes that "all that remained alive and indestructible of Christianity in me" has reasserted itself. Cleansed at last of the grime of Marxism he feels a "sense of well-being, even of physical well-being, and of strength and courage of which I did not believe myself capable."

Spina's reconversion to Christianity involves nothing so simple as a return to the faith of his childhood; he has no intention of embracing the institutional Church. He agrees with Don Benedetto that "the spirit of the Lord has abandoned the Church, which has become a formal, conventional, materialistic institution, obsessed with worldly and caste worries. . . ." Spina will have his religion back, but only on his own terms, for it will be "denuded of all mythology, of all theology, of all Church control." Angered by the Pope's failure to declare war on Fascism, Spina rejects institutional Christianity in its entirety. He slashes away at the "mythology" and "theology" to create a gospel comprised of the ethical imperatives of the Sermon on the Mount, the elevation of the human at the expense of the divine and a this-worldly salvation that commits one to the struggle against injustice. "If we apply our moral feelings to the disorder that reigns about us", Spina confides to his journal, "we cannot remain inactive and console ourselves by looking forward to another, supernatural world. The evil that we have to combat is not that sad abstraction called the devil, but everything that sets man against man. . . ."

From the vantage point of an insider Silone saw clearly the inadequacies of Marxism; for the clarity of his vision Christians owe him much. But his rejection of the primacy of eternal salvation should give pause to all who believe that Christ died for something other than a man-made utopia, even one constructed in the name of the Lord. I can walk a good way with Ignazio Silone, but then with regret I must part company with him, for I refuse to cast aside that "mythology" which gives transcendence to the Christian life. Still, Silone took at least part of Christ's message seriously; he ached for an end to the brutalities that plague human existence, brutalities that the Church has at times failed to oppose with sufficient vigor. Silone loved his fellow man and he loved the Christ of the Sermon on the Mount; though he rejected the institutional Church, he also refused the easy consolation that the secular reformer finds in atheism and materialism. Was he any less a Christian than those professed followers of Christ who declined

—out of complacency, fear, or perhaps, even secret approval—to oppose the malignant power of Italian Fascism? The Lord demands much of one and Ignazio Silone gave much; orthodox Christians would be foolish to ignore his testimony.

VI

CHARLES WILLIAMS'

War in Heaven

"The telephone was ringing wildly, but without result, since there was no one in the room but the corpse." With a smile of recognition one settles back comfortably upon reading such an opening sentence; obviously it will lead into one of those deliciously witty and urbane British murder mysteries peopled with supercilious butlers, eccentric dowagers and slightly lunatic lords. One problem: the title of the book, *War in Heaven*, sounds too serious; surely something snappier would better catch the browsing eye in search of light bedtime fare. The mystery buff's perplexity deepens as he follows the investigations of the intrepid Inspector Colquhoun, an impeccably English sleuth who pursues his ratiocinations over a cup of steaming tea. In exasperation the Assistant Commissioner of Police exclaims: "What an infernally religious case this is getting!" This worthy public servant understates the matter considerably: this "infernally religious case" leads one slyly from the opening sentence to a final clash between good and evil that propels *War in Heaven* into the ranks of genuine Christian classics. It should come as no surprise that this novel defies neat classification, for if anyone ever deserved the label *sui generis* Charles Williams certainly does.

Williams led a fairly uneventful life as an employee of the London office of Oxford University Press from 1908 until his death in 1945. The outward routine of a valued employee of the Press supplied only a thin veneer to the inner life of a man possessed of one of the richest, most fertile—and, at times, downright bizarre—imaginations I have ever encountered. By 1930, when *War in Heaven* (the first of his seven novels) appeared, Williams, a devout if sometimes unorthodox Anglican, had dabbled in Rosicrucianism and had penetrated deeply into the esoteric reaches of black magic with something more than the scholar's curiosity. His quest to fathom the mystic knowledge of both Christianity and the black arts created in Williams a profound sense of the reality of the supernatural; for Williams the natural and supernatural existed side by side, often spilling over into one another and leaving the man of acute discernment sharply aware of the intermingling of the two realms. Small wonder that J. R. R. Tolkien once termed Williams (as recounted in Humphrey Carpenter's book *The Inklings*) a "witch doctor".

Lest one be scared off by Tolkien's gibe one should note that Williams won the respect and devoted friendship of C. S. Lewis, who saw in Williams' outpouring of fiction, poetry, literary criticism and theology the distinguishing marks of a powerful Christian mind.

War in Heaven demonstrates well the workings of that mind. At the center of the novel stands the Archdeacon of Fardles, a "round, dapper little cleric in gaiters", who discovers quite accidentally and much to his bemusement that the battered old communion cup stored in a cupboard in his church is the Holy Graal, the chalice Christ offered to his disciples at the Last Supper. As a commonsensical man the Archdeacon refuses to be prostrated with awe. "In one sense, of course," he muses, "the Graal is unimportant—it is a symbol less near reality now than any chalice of consecrated wine." Enter Gregory Persimmons, a thoroughly despicable retired publisher of books on black magic who enjoys entering "into those lives which he touched and twist[ing] them out of their security into a sliding destruction." Gregory lusts after the Graal with a drooling obsessiveness; he would pervert the sacred object into a weapon of destruction and unspeakable evil. The Archdeacon bridles at such outrageous perversity: "There are decencies. There is a way of behaving in these things. And the Graal, if it is the Graal . . . was not meant for the greedy orgies of a delirious tomtit." Kenneth Mornington, an employee in Gregory's publishing house who views the Graal through the mists of "exalted poetry and the high romantic tradition in literature", and the Duke of the North Ridings, a Roman Catholic who wishes to deposit the Graal safely in the Vatican, complete the band of slightly ludicrous "knights" sworn to save the holy vessel from Gregory's clutches.

I shall not recount the particulars that attend the madcap pursuit back and forth between Fardles and London, nor shall I reveal the startling but deeply satisfying denouement. Should not the aficionado of the murder mystery be allowed to dig out those nuggets for himself? The Christian implications of *War in Heaven* do, however, deserve further notice. Williams' achievement reaches its peak in his stunning ability to render frighteningly palpable the evil that stalks the earth. Our era stands in dire need of such a message. Just as the modern world's conception of goodness has been watered down and sentimentalized to the point of banality, so has its perception of the dark and brooding powers that lurk beyond the periphery of the visible world been reduced to a silly fascination with the trappings of the occult. Modern man readily agrees with

Inspector Colquhoun that "the devil was something in which children believed, but which was
generally known not to exist, certainly not as
taking any active part in the affairs of the world."
One must beware of slipping into a preoccupation
with the Prince of Darkness, especially in the form
of positing a dualistic universe in which good and
evil—God and Satan—battle on equal terms. Does
one necessarily flirt with heresy, however, to suggest that modern man, in his enlightened disbelief
in Satan, has removed from his world the ultimate
source of the daily horror that lies as near as the
morning newspaper? Whole libraries packed to
the ceiling with tomes on social pathology and
psychological imbalance will not explain—at least
not to me—the origins of Gregory Persimmons'
"rapture in the worship of treachery and malice
and cruelty and sin." Satan exists, even if we
refuse to acknowledge that fact while skipping
blithely around the edge of the Pit, and Charles
Williams forces one in *War in Heaven* to contemplate the enormity and awesomeness of the
forces of evil. Modern man could well take a
long draught from the cup that Charles Williams
proffers.

VII

EMIL BRUNNER'S

The Theology of Crisis

Several years ago when I embarked on an attempt to educate myself in theology a friend of mine warned only half-jokingly: "Never trust a theologian with a German name." Nothing I read in Martin Luther verified my friend's remark; I rather liked much of what I found in the writings of the rebellious Augustinian monk. The German thinkers of the nineteenth century moved me closer to agreement with my friend's *caveat*, for here I encountered a succession of writers who seemed intent upon burying Christian supernaturalism under an avalanche of rationalist scholarship. Then I discovered such scholars as Albrecht Ritschl and Adolf von Harnack who laid the foundations of a social gospel that in the twentieth century would reduce liberal Christianity to the "praying wing" of the secular reform movement. Not until my reading carried me into the twentieth century, however, did I grasp the wisdom in the warning that had been offered; Rudolf Bultmann and Paul Tillich were definitely not to be trusted. I might have blamed it all on the Protestants had not Father Hans Küng's writings come under my scrutiny; even Catholics with German names were untrustworthy guides to the historic truths of Christianity.

There remained two key figures whose work I had not yet read. I had heard mixed comments on Karl Barth and Emil Brunner. Barth, for example, had first come to my attention through Reinhold Niebuhr, the one German-named religious thinker whom I did trust. Yet the Evangelical writer Francis Schaeffer counted Barth among the prime villains in the subversion of Christian truth. Further reason to include Barth and his colleague Brunner in the rogue's gallery of modern theologians came from the Roman Catholic philosopher Frederick Wilhelmsen who, in his book on Hilaire Belloc, assails the Swiss theologians for creating a "Barbarian God of the peat bogs". Wilhelmsen piqued my interest; such a God sounded infinitely more attractive than Bultmann's demythologized Christ or Tillich's "New Being". With a certain perverse curiosity I decided to read Brunner's *The Theology of Crisis*.

In 1928 Emil Brunner, a professor of theology at the University of Zurich, crossed the Atlantic to deliver the Swander Lectures at the seminary of the Reformed Church in Lancaster, Pennsylvania.

Brunner arrived as an evangel, for he and Barth had already been hailed—and damned—as two of the leading proponents of the new "crisis" or "dialectical" theology, more commonly known in America as "neo-orthodoxy". Brunner left behind a Europe still suffering the ravages of the Great War, a conflagration that had consumed the bourgeois dream of a dawning (if not already arrived) era of peace, prosperity and progress. Liberal Protestantism, in part the brainchild of German thinkers, had been shattered; where amidst the bloodshed and carnage could one find justification for the hope of a gradual ushering in of the Kingdom of God on earth? By 1928 Brunner had taken the full measure of this chimera and had shouldered the task of providing Christians with a "realistic understanding of life". Against this backdrop he came to the lectern in Lancaster "to introduce to the English-speaking world the theology of crisis." A year later Charles Scribner's Sons published Brunner's lectures in book form.

Those readers in search of soothing words should avoid Brunner's book, for he paints a somber picture of the plight of sinful man. He disdains those warm, laving waters of sentimentality in which some Christians love to immerse themselves; he seizes the sinner by the nape of the neck and plunges him into the frigid waters of an Alpine pool. The shock may be fatal, but if one survives, one's sensibilities will definitely be invigorated. Brunner strips Christians of all reassuring talk of divine immanence, human goodness and a benign God. Man's much-vaunted rational powers quail before Brunner's stern gaze: "This pride, this claim of reason to be the court of last appeal, the supreme judge of truth, constitutes sin; it is the heart of sin." Man loudly proclaims his goodness, intelligence and achievements, but his words echo hollowly, for God, "the Other One, the mysterious and unknowable One", remains unmoved by man's preening and strutting. This God reveals himself only "by 'piercing' into the world"; he takes possession of the sinner *when* and *because* he wills to do so.

Wilhelmsen may be on to something: this does sound like a pre-Christian god of the peat bogs. There is more, however: Brunner does not leave man groveling before a God of frightening and unapproachable majesty. He holds out a promise that harks back to the Protestant Reformers of the sixteenth century: "By faith ye are saved." "Repentance", says Brunner, "means a radical turning away from self-reliance to trust in God alone." Through the revelation in Jesus Christ, through the atoning death of the Word made Flesh, God unveils to man the Truth and the Way to eternal life. "God in his mercy . . . throw[s] a bridge across the chasm between himself and

man and . . . blaze[s] a trail where man himself
cannot go." In his despair, "with the passion of a
drowning man", the sinner grasps the hand which
God extends to him.

Brunner urges the destruction of that "colossal
ideology" which since the Enlightenment of the
eighteenth century has tantalized Western man
with the promise that good and reasonable human
beings will march onward to temporal perfection.
Brunner singles out for special condemnation the
Christian fellow travelers of this secular doctrine,
those liberals and social gospelers for whom "the
pastor's study . . . has become transformed into
an office for numerous social agencies; and the
sermon is a piece of applied popular ethics as the
day requires it." No otherworldly quietism for
Brunner, though; he understands that the man of
faith—he who has recognized his own helplessness
without God—will embrace this world of suffering
and seek to mitigate injustice: "But he will never
confuse this sphere of relative human progress and
betterment with the Kingdom of God."

Americans of 1928 were not inclined to look
kindly upon Brunner's talk of the despair that lies
at the heart of man's existence. They might have
surmised that this Teutonic merchant of gloom
had read too much Schopenhauer and Spengler
or had seen one-too-many Wagnerian operas.
Who was he to dispel the feverish optimism that

gripped America in the 1920s? Had not the United States emerged from World War I as the most powerful nation in the world? Were not science, technology and ingenuity enabling Americans to project an ever-brightening future for humankind? If Brunner wished to chant a tale of woe and despair then he should do it to the worn-out, dying lands of Europe, not to this exuberant young nation now coming into its own.

Fifty years have taught us much; perhaps it is time to hearken to Emil Brunner's words. We are weak, we sin, we despair; progress brings new difficulties, material abundance leaves us sated but unsatisfied, our optimism falters and the world grows ever more insecure. Only Brunner's "Other One, the mysterious and unknowable One" can save us from the mess we have made of the creation that came from his hand.

VIII

SIGRID UNDSET'S

Kristin Lavransdatter

The Lord moves in mysterious ways. He uses
even the damned mob of female readers (to para-
phrase Nathaniel Hawthorne's comment on the
women writers of his day) to accomplish his ends.
In recent years major publishing houses and busy
little feminist presses have dredged up virtually
every scrap of paper ever scribbled upon by a
would-be woman writer. The result: myriad
volumes of torpid prose and jejune lucubrations
have descended upon the booksellers, to be grabbed
from the shelves by earnest feminists in search
of solace and inspiration. I shudder whenever I
encounter one of these freshly printed "classics"
glaring at me from the bookracks; I think of the
many readers who will brush aside the writings of
such "sexist" authors as Fitzgerald and Hemingway
to plod through the self-pitying lamentations of
their oppressed sisters.

The twists and turns and ironies of human
existence appear at the least expected moments.

Witness, in this case, the recent publication in a mass-market edition of Sigrid Undset's magisterial novel of fourteenth-century Norway, *Kristin Lavransdatter*. I recently spied the book (published in three volumes, each bearing the portrait of a Liv Ullmann look-alike) reposing in a special display with such titles as *The Male Enemy* and *You Too Can Be a Weightlifter*. Closer scrutiny revealed that a local feminist reading group had singled out *Kristin Lavransdatter* as a Topic for Discussion. I suspect that these ladies had heard that Sigrid Undset recounts a harrowing tale of female oppression amidst the Nordic snows. Because of medieval Norway's unenlightened divorce laws, Kristin drags through life encumbered with an insensitive husband and seven unruly brats (all boys). A repressive society drives Ms. Lavransdatter into a convent instead of allowing her to flee to Oslo to pursue a liberated lifestyle.

Kristin Lavransdatter may propel feminists to new heights of outrage, but it also happens to be one of the supreme achievements of the Christian artistic sensibility and, in addition, one of the most masterful novels of the twentieth century. Sigrid Undset, winner of the Nobel Prize for literature in 1928, traces the progress of a wayfaring pilgrim through the sin-steeped morass of this world. Though set in the fourteenth century, the novel attains a timelessness that characterizes the monuments of Christian art. Whether the fourth century of St. Augustine's wrestling with the flesh or the twentieth century of Graham Greene's despair-ridden protagonists, the message remains the same: with God's help sinners can find their way to Glory. Few writers have better plumbed the depths of travail of a soul clutched by sin yet hungering after righteousness than Sigrid Undset.

The mystery of God's grace and the power of his love first come to young Kristin through her father, Lavrans Björgulfsön, who as a youth had longed to serve God in the cloister, and from Brother Edvin, a saintly mendicant and traveling soul winner who instructs his countrymen in the ways of God's goodness. Kristin's childhood schooling in godliness founders on the shoals of the passions of young womanhood. She defies her father to marry Erlend Nikulaussön, a high-spirited and reckless nobleman who before meeting Kristin had stolen another man's wife, lived with her in adulterous union and fathered two bastards upon her.

With the blindness and inexperience of youth Kristin believes that her love for Erlend—and his for her—promises a life of undiluted bliss. Erlend's long-neglected estates flourish under Kristin's guidance and son after son fills the great hall at Husaby with the laughing chaos of childhood. Erlend soon begins to chafe under the strictures of domesticity. His restlessness and discontent lead him ultimately into a disastrous plot against the Crown. Kristin's remorse and guilt over her willfulness toward her beloved father plague her and a vindictive bitterness toward Erlend festers in her heart. She learns that "the devil's work is that which begins in sweet desire and ends in them that work it stinging and biting each other like toad and asp." As the hammer blows of sorrow fall upon her—Erlend's dalliance with another woman, the death of Kristin's parents, Erlend's violent end and the loss of her sons through death and adulthood—Kristin gains in spiritual depth what she loses in temporal happiness. As an aging woman, shorn of family and possessions, she realizes that "the life of the body was tainted with unrest beyond all cure; in the world where men mixed, begot new generations, were driven together by fleshly love, and loved their own flesh, there came heart-ache and broken hopes, as surely as rime comes in autumn; both life and death sundered friends at last, as surely as winter parts the tree from its leaves."

Seized by the love of God welling in her heart, Kristin, now approaching fifty years of age, enters a convent, and here at last she finds surcease from sorrow. In the quiet and solitude of the cloister she reflects upon her life; she remembers the joy, accepts the pain and realizes that God has guided her footsteps through the tribulations that beset the pilgrim. The bitterness and guilt that had poisoned the wellsprings of her heart disappear and the healing balm of God's grace suffuses her soul. She at last understands the words she has repeated since childhood: "Forgive us our trespasses as we forgive those who trespass against us."

The Black Plague sweeps over Norway and Kristin contracts it while selflessly ministering to its victims. As she lies upon her deathbed she removes her wedding ring to give it to the Church to support Masses for the dead. Through the mists of approaching death Kristin sees that the configuration of the ring has left a small "M" imprinted upon her finger—"M", Mary, the Virgin Mother of Christ: "Under the glittering golden ring a mark had been set secretly upon her, showing that she was his handmaid, owned by the Lord and King who was now coming, borne by the priest's anointed hands, to give her freedom and salvation."

Both in fourteenth-century Norway and in twentieth-century America the Lord moves in mysterious ways. Some young feminist, filled with rage at the real and imagined slights of a fallen social order, may happen upon *Kristin Lavransdatter* and find in its pages the message of redemptive love that enables God's creatures to transcend the narrow confines of the quest for earthly justice. I hope the members of the local feminist reading circle waded through all one thousand pages of *Kristin Lavransdatter*: they may have discovered a liberation far greater than they had ever imagined.

IX

JOHN HENRY NEWMAN'S

Apologia pro Vita Sua

I have an inkling of how Daniel must have felt in the lions' den. I am not an Anglican, yet I am about to launch into an essay on John Henry Newman's *Apologia pro Vita Sua* with the knowledge that my many Anglo-Catholic friends will bridle at the thought of profane hands laying hold upon one of their nineteenth-century heroes. While these Anglo-Catholics have steeped themselves in Newman's writings, I have only recently begun to read his books. To compound my temerity I intend not only to write of Newman the Anglo-Catholic but also to praise him for abandoning the Anglican communion to embrace the Catholicism of Rome.

The *Apologia*, published in 1864, charts Newman's famous, and often painful, spiritual odyssey. Born in 1801, Newman came of age in an English church caught in the throes of theological change and controversy. The Evangelicals sought to claim

the church as their own by emphasizing the
Protestant elements in Anglicanism and by quash-
ing "creeping Romanism". The rising tide of
Liberalism, a movement that would sweep through
the ranks of Protestantism in the nineteenth century, found recruits within the Anglicanism of
Newman's day; then—as now—Christians fell
prey to the temptation of, in Newman's words,
"subjecting to human judgment those revealed
doctrines which are in their nature beyond and
independent of it." Newman himself felt the pull
of Liberalism in the 1820s, but by the end of the
decade he had successfully resisted the allurements
of the "anti-dogmatic principle".

In the 1830s Newman joined John Keble, Richard
Hurrell Froude and Edward Pusey to combat
Liberalism and to provide an Anglican Catholic
alternative to Evangelicalism. Newman poured
his energies into the resulting Oxford or Tractarian
Movement and in defense of Anglicanism's *via
media* between Rome and Geneva he immersed
himself in the study of Anglican theology, the
writings of the Church Fathers and the various
doctrinal controversies that had wracked Christianity in its early years. Newman patiently bore
the charges of "papistry" hurled at him by his
opponents, for he knew that he harbored no desire
to betray Anglicanism into the hands of the pope.

Newman confirmed the suspicions of his critics when in 1841 he published his controversial *Tract XC* in which he argued for the compatibility of the Thirty-nine Articles with Roman Catholic doctrine. For this effrontery he earned the condemnation of the Anglican bishops.

Newman's increasing disillusionment with Anglicanism led him to turn his back on Canterbury and to set his course reluctantly and fitfully toward Rome. His sadness at leaving his former faith should console Anglo-Catholics as well as chasten those Roman Catholics inclined to gloat over the capture of such a prize as Newman. For several years Newman found himself mired "in a state of moral sickness, neither able to acquiesce in Anglicanism, nor able to go to Rome." His integrity and high sense of duty prevented him from throwing himself hastily into the arms of the Roman Catholic Church; he needed assurance, the kind that comes only through rigorous study and intellectual conviction. He refused to beat his breast in public or to whine of his plight to his friends; in the solitude of his own chamber he wrestled with the decision that had to be made. In late 1843 he resigned the vicarage of St. Mary's Church in Oxford, but still he dangled in the limbo of spiritual indecision. A year later he vowed to resolve once and for all the questions that continued to plague him. Convinced at last he became a Roman Catholic in 1845. For Newman this "was like coming into port after a rough sea"; he had come home for good this time and from the perspective of 1864 he could write of his decision: "I have been in perfect peace and contentment; I never have had one doubt."

Christians of other persuasions convert to Roman Catholicism for a variety of reasons. The tangled skein of motives that lead to conversion often leaves the theologian perplexed and exasperated. Psychologists and sociologists gladly step in to supply answers, for they delight in reducing the convert to a quivering mass of neuroses and social maladjustments. One need not adhere to such reductionism to agree that the phenomenon of religious conversion cannot be attributed solely to the sudden flash of doctrinal conviction. Some converts to Roman Catholicism seek the womb-like comfort of rigid authority (or at least they did in the pre-Vatican II "dark ages" of the Church); others see the Church as a bastion of traditional moral values in an age of fecklessness and decay; still others delight in a sense of awe and mystery that sends shivers up their formerly Protestant spines. Some embrace the Roman Church out of a perverse desire to be different, to shock family and friends and to trumpet their liberation from the traditions in which they were raised. The most novel interpretation of conversion comes from the

literary critic and radical polemicist Philip Rahv.
In Eileen Simpson's book *Poets in Their Youth* she
recalls that Rahv once explained to her why so
many American writers had become Catholics in
the 1940s; they were, said Rahv, searching for new
metaphors. Newman would have been appalled
by such variegated and often trivial motives; he reduced the matter to utter simplicity: "The simple
question is: Can *I* (it is personal, not whether
another, but can *I*) be saved in the English church?
Am *I* in safety, were I to die tonight? Is it a mortal
sin in *me*, not joining another communion?"

My Anglo-Catholic friends can relax; I am not
about to insist that they rush to the nearest Roman
Catholic church and beg for admission lest the
flames of hellfire begin to scorch their sinful
Anglican souls. I do not believe that Newman
intended such an inference to be drawn from his
Apologia. Still, the seriousness and intensity of
his relentless pursuit of the truth shock those
Christians who denigrate the importance of cor-
rect doctrine. The Liberalism that Newman fought
in his day has done its work well; the "anti-
dogmatic principle" has convinced more than one
Christian that the faith can be reduced to a warm
glow in the center of one's heart. Newman stands
as a rebuke to such a watered-down version of
Christianity; he challenges one to seek the truth
with mind and heart and to submit one's self to it.
Dare any Christian ignore his example?

X

FRANÇOIS MAURIAC'S

Life of Jesus

"The age of fairy tales has passed. Let's put to rest once and for all this fanciful talk of the divinity of that ragged Jew who wandered the fringes of the Roman Empire and got himself nailed to a cross for his irksomeness. God come to this earth? Nonsense! How could anyone of even moderate intelligence believe such rubbish?"

Any Christian who moves in circles that exalt the intellect stripped of "superstition" and "outmoded" beliefs has probably felt the sting of such a rebuke. Satan marshalls his forces with the skill of a master strategist and the Prince of Darkness knows that the appeal to reason has set the corrosive acids of doubt to work upon many a Christian. At times it appears that Satan's minions have gained the ascendancy in the war against Christianity. But the gates of hell shall not prevail and if perverted intellect savages the Gospel, so too does God raise up his champions.

François Mauriac, the French Roman Catholic novelist who won the Nobel Prize for literature in 1952, belongs to this company. In 1936, still smarting from the attacks of fellow Catholics who had condemned his fiction as pornographic, Mauriac published his *Life of Jesus*. While his biography of Christ may have placated his critics within the Church, it won him few plaudits in the world of letters, for the book appeared in the heart of the "Red Decade", an era in which the Marxist vision of a heaven on earth had seized the imaginations of large numbers of Western intellectuals. On every side Mauriac saw men prostrating themselves before the god of the dialectic; eschewing Marxism's promise of earthly salvation Mauriac turned instead to the humble Galilean who 1900 years before had pierced to the core of the human tragedy: "What defiles man does not come from without; he is the maker of his own defilement; it is bred in his own heart and is the fruit of his own lust." The intellectuals of today wish to hear such words no more than did their predecessors of the 1930s.

Mauriac must have known that the men of learning of his day would either ignore or belittle the *Life of Jesus*. Had not that same class of men reacted similarly to Christ himself when he made his incarnate way through the world of the first century? Mauriac reminds one that since the time of Christ men of the most acute intellectual discernment have frequently rejected the message borne to this earth by the Son of God. Jesus Christ "dressed the truth in stories so simple that the learned did not understand them." What blocked their comprehension? Mauriac replies with words he imagines that the Lord might have addressed to those men of his day who were puffed with pride over the profundity and incisiveness of their own intellects: "I am not a God of logic. There is nothing farther from me than all your philosophy. My heart has its reasons which escape your reason, because I am Love."

Mauriac here reiterates a truth set forth in the seventeenth century by Blaise Pascal, one of Mauriac's spiritual guides. Some Christians worry needlessly over the judgments passed upon their faith by secular intellectuals. How many times has one heard a Christian, stung by the gibes of his antagonists, retort by proudly listing the men and women of puissant intellect who have followed the tried and true path of Christian orthodoxy? What does that prove? Does that authenticate the Gospel? If one surveyed the leading thinkers of the West since the Enlightenment, one would probably discover that those on the side of unbelief and heterodoxy would form a substantial majority. God's cause does not wax and wane according to the number of Nobel Prize winners in his camp. The scribes and scholars of Palestine rejected Christ, but "the Son of Man found himself on a common footing with sinners, with publicans, with lost women", and with, one might add, fishermen, carpenters and other humble folk possessed of no scholarly credentials. One hesitates to pursue this line of thought too far, for it only encourages those Christians who seldom miss a chance to pour kerosene on the fires of anti-intellectualism. Still, the question must be asked: does a Ph.D. degree guarantee to lead one unerringly through the Gates of Glory? Admitting that God has vested man with a mind capable of fathoming many truths, one still finds it difficult to gainsay Mauriac's belief that "happy are those who can close their eyes and, with the abandonment of a child, cling to his garment with all their strength."

Why did the unlettered turn so readily to Jesus Christ? Quite simple, Mauriac answers: Here stood no pale abstraction, no god of the metaphysicians, but a God of flesh and blood who, though he transcended the humanity of mankind, fully embodied that humanity. With the humility of one unafraid of the inexplicable, Mauriac bows his head before this mystery: fully man yet fully God. Those intent upon elucidating the humanity of Christ frequently fall into the trap of portraying a mousy being possessed of all the vigor of one's valetudinarian maiden aunt. Mauriac by contrast presents the *true* humanity of the Savior; he renders "a Jesus misunderstood and therefore irritated, impatient, sometimes raging, as is all love." A Christ of passion, of vitality and, yes, at times, of violence: "But beneath this surface violence, there reigned a deep peace which was his own and which was like no other."

Try as one might to understand Jesus Christ, man's flawed and truncated powers of intellection finally bar one from penetrating to the innermost recesses of the God-man. In this age of rationalism, scientism and prideful technological expertise man seeks knowledge to gain mastery, but the figure of Jesus Christ eludes his grasp. That does not matter to François Mauriac; for him Christ remains the "God who lies in wait" on the road to Damascus, waiting for Saul of Tarsus, waiting for you, waiting for me.

XI

WILL D. CAMPBELL'S

Brother to a Dragonfly

Challenged once to define the essence of Christianity in no more than ten words, Will Campbell, a Baptist preacher from Mississippi, replied (as he recounts in his autobiography, *Brother to a Dragonfly*): "We're all bastards but God loves us anyway."

One doubts that theologians will rush to incorporate Preacher Will's definition into their treatises. But then Campbell is no theologian; in fact, by his own admission he did not even become a Christian until long after he had begun to preach the Gospel. Although Will Campbell delivered his first sermon while still in high school, thereby earning the right at the tender age of sixteen "to buy Coca-Colas at clergy discount", it took many years and much experience before he could honestly call himself a Christian.

To all outward appearances Campbell served his Lord and his fellow man diligently and well in those "pre-Christian" years. Even as a boy in Amite County, Mississippi, he had been marked as one destined to fill a pulpit, if for no other reasons than his scrawniness and ability to offer a good grace at mealtime. After his youthful initiation into the ministry he served in the Pacific during World War II and then studied at Wake Forest College and Yale Divinity School. In 1954, with two years of preaching in a Baptist church in Louisiana behind him, he became Director of Religious Life at the University of Mississippi. A normal man might have settled down to a pleasant routine of arranging weeks of religious emphasis, counseling students, sipping mint juleps (Preacher Will belongs to the imbibing wing of Southern Baptists) and savoring the unhurried life of a Southern university town. Will Campbell was no ordinary man; besides, the times were out of joint: in the year of his arrival at Ole Miss the Supreme Court of the United States declared in the Brown decision that racial segregation had outlived its time. Campbell had already advanced far beyond most of his fellow Southern whites in his thinking on race; while stationed in the Pacific he had read Howard Fast's *Freedom Road*, a novel which details the struggles of freed slaves after the Civil War. The book shocked him from complacency and led to a "conversion experience comparable to none I had ever had, and I knew it would have to find expression." Campbell's readiness to act upon his new awareness soon led to his departure from the University and to interracial work for the National Council of Churches, an activity that won him nationwide fame as the conscience of the white South and notoriety among his own people as a "nigger-loving" Judas Iscariot.

That he became proud and smug can be forgiven him. He had escaped rural poverty on the strength of intelligence and initiative; he had become a celebrity, far removed from his ignorant kinsmen who were venting their anger in brutal acts upon blacks. Will Campbell had set himself up for a fall, a fall—as it turned out—into grace. On an afternoon in August of 1965 Preacher Will—enlightened Southerner, champion of the Gospel and crusading liberal—sat in a "heavily mortgaged house in Fairhope, Alabama", draining cans of beer with "two of the most troubled men I have ever known". One was P. D. East— owner of the house, exiled Mississippi journalist, illegitimate son of a Delta belle, author of *The Magnolia Jungle* and renegade Methodist; the other was Joseph Lee Campbell, Will's brother, now far gone on amphetamines and the debilitating wear of a chaotic life. These two men taught Will a lesson that day: they revealed to him what it means to be a Christian.

Will had just learned that his friend Jonathan Daniels, an Episcopal seminarian who had come to Alabama to help blacks register to vote, had been slain in Hayneville by a deputy sheriff named Thomas Coleman. P. D. East, his normal audaciousness swollen by large quantities of hops, decided to test Will's definition of Christianity. Campbell had no difficulty in agreeing that God loved Jonathan Daniels and that Thomas Coleman was a wretched bastard. But P. D. forced Will to reverse the terms: Jonathan was a bastard and God loved Thomas. Through the haze of beer, grief and frayed emotions Will experienced his second conversion, one far more profound than that provoked by Howard Fast's novel: Will Campbell became a Christian.

I was laughing at myself [Campbell writes], at twenty years of a ministry which had become, without my realizing it, a ministry of liberal sophistication. An attempted negation of Jesus, of human engineering, of riding the coattails of Caesar, of playing on his ballpark, by his rules and with his ball, of looking to government to make and verify and authenticate our morality, of worshiping at the shrine of enlightenment and academia, of making an idol of the Supreme Court, a theology of law and order and of denying not only the faith I professed to hold but my history and my people—the Thomas Colemans.

It had not been easy for a Mississippi farm boy to admit the full equality of blacks; it had been even harder, and had taken many more years, for a man of impeccable liberal views to understand that the Son of God died to redeem rednecks, crackers, woolhats and Kluxers—the Thomas Colemans of this world.

Will Campbell's newfound insight did not bring him joy, comfort or the praises of the world. His insistent support of black rights ensured the continued hostility of his fellow white Mississippians, while his ministry to Klansmen won him the obloquy of self-righteous Northern liberals. His beloved brother Joe, the "dragonfly" in Will's life, continued his deathly spiral into the depths of addiction to amphetamines and Seconal. Even Will's gospel of love and redemption and reconciliation could not save Joe from the demons that rode his back. While Will pursued his tumultuous ministry to blacks and rednecks in the late 1960s he watched helplessly as Joe drove on to destruction. Like the dragonfly, that "quintessence of speed and motion and restlessness", Joe too "one day, with the same swiftness and suddenness and sureness of flight . . . drop[ped] to the earth", dead of a massive coronary.

If *Brother to a Dragonfly* chronicles Will Campbell's discovery of the true meaning of the Gospel, it also reveals his awakening to "the sadness of human existence, the depth and complexity of human sin, the nature of humanity in microcosm."

Will Campbell has come a long way from that skinny sixteen-year-old who forty years ago first entered the pulpit of a country church in Mississippi. He has learned about life and death, about blacks and whites, about love and hatred; but most of all, he has learned that despite our dubious parentage, "God loves us anyway."

XII

DOROTHY DAY'S

The Long Loneliness

Dorothy Day irritates me. She stabs at my conscience and refuses to let me rest easy in the life I lead. She chides me when I buy a new sports coat, scolds me when I purchase an automobile and shakes her head disapprovingly when I sit down to an especially abundant dinner. She nags me about the homeless, the hungry and the naked—those destitute men, women and children who hover on the edge of my world, loved of God but despised of man. Miss Day is welcome to her Christianity, but must she be so literal? She takes those New Testament injunctions so seriously. If someone snatched up her coat she would chase after him and force her cloak upon him as well. That carries matters too far. I have worked hard for my possessions; why should I give them to the lazy, the shiftless and the no-account?

Dorothy Day will not relent and my conscience will not slink off to its appointed corner. It would be easier to ignore her if she did not have such formidable allies, but Christ backs her up and a long line of godly Christians from St. Francis to Mother Teresa of Calcutta range themselves on her side. For some fifty years, while the rest of us have busied ourselves in getting ahead, Dorothy Day has devoted her life to the losers of New York's skid row; through the Catholic Worker Movement she has made the acts of mercy a daily reality. She is old now, a woman in her eighties, and she wears the seamed and lined face of one who has suffered much for those who suffer.[1] She can rest secure in the knowledge that she has faithfully followed the words of Christ: "Inasmuch as ye have done it unto one of the least of these my brethren, ye have done it unto me."

Those who know only the Dorothy Day of the Catholic Workers may be shocked by some of the revelations in her autobiography, *The Long Loneliness*. Could this saintly white-haired grandmother actually have spent many a long night carousing in a New York bar fondly known to its habitués as the "Hell Hole"? Yes, and more; as a young woman she gladly yielded to the temptations of the flesh. Dorothy Day came of age in the New York City of World War I, a time and place in which the young people of America's

---

[1] Although Dorothy Day died in late 1981, I have deliberately left this passage in its original present tense; surely in the deepest sense Miss Day remains with us.

hinterlands gathered to exult in the sensual vibrancy of their youthfulness and to plunge into the surging currents of political and social radicalism. Greenwich Village offered much to a young idealist with a craving for excitement. One could see Eugene O'Neill, his heart full of the poetry and anguish he would pour into his plays, drinking with his friends; or hear Max Eastman, the handsome socialist journalist, arguing politics and literature; or dream of following the dashing John Reed into the maelstrom of revolution. The staid Episcopalianism of Miss Day's upbringing hadn't a chance in competition with the Village; she turned her back disdainfully on the mildly pious Christians of her former life. The young radicals, with their high spirits, dedication and *joie de vivre*, entranced young Dorothy Day, and she surrendered herself to a life in which radical dreams mingled with the sweet gratification of the senses.

Politics and dissipation failed to blot out a worshipfulness that skirted the edges of Miss Day's consciousness and surged forth at inopportune times. Frequently after sessions at the "Hell Hole" she found herself on her knees in St. Joseph's Church, "warmed and comforted by the lights and silence, the kneeling people and the atmosphere of worship." Only after her conversion would she fully realize why she had slipped away from her drinking companions to seek brief moments of refuge in that church. "People have so great a need to reverence, to worship, to adore; it is a psychological necessity of human nature." In the course of the 1920s Miss Day crept closer and closer to the Roman Catholic Church. She prayed, attended Mass and read Pascal and the Spanish mystics, St. Teresa of Avila and St. John of the Cross. Living in a beach cottage on Staten Island with her common-law husband, Forster, she felt a peace and happiness she had never experienced. But just as Dante's love for Beatrice drew him upward toward the Beatific Vision, so Dorothy Day's devotion to Forster beckoned her to a higher love. "I was happy but my very happiness made me know that there was a greater happiness to be obtained from life than any I had ever known. I began to think, to weigh things, and it was at this time that I began consciously to pray more."

Dorothy Day's love for Forster bore fruit in the person of a tiny gift from God, a daughter whom she named Tamar. But at this very moment of ineffable joy, sadness began to stir in Miss Day's heart; she knew that her decision to have Tamar baptized and to enter the Church herself would be realized only at the price of her union with Forster. The sincerity of his convictions—his principled atheism and anarchism—made marriage and a family life within the Church impossible for him. To follow Christ sometimes breaks one's heart. The happiness offered by the world often conflicts with the demands of disciplehood. Dorothy Day chose the hard road of renunciation; she and Tamar entered the Church and Forster left. Sorrow and loss lacerated her heart; from this travail came a painful knowledge: one pays a price to follow the Lord.

Miss Day's conversion bewildered her radical friends. How could she betray her principles to join a Church that "was lined up with property, with the wealthy, with the state, with capitalism, with all the forces of reaction"? Despite the misgivings of her friends Miss Day clung to her vision of a just social order, but not until she met Peter Maurin in 1932 could she completely reconcile the spiritual truth of Roman Catholicism with her commitment to radical activism. Peter Maurin, French peasant, common laborer and "a troubador of Christ, singing solutions to the world's ills", led her to the path she would follow the rest of her life. His joyful embrace of Lady Poverty and his selfless devotion to the creation of a society "in which it is easier for people to be good" furnished the inspiration and guidance Dorothy Day needed. Together they founded the Catholic Worker Movement to minister to society's rejects and to work for a better world. On May 1, 1933, the first issue of *The Catholic Worker* appeared in New York's Union Square.

Dorothy Day fused her love of God with compassion for the Savior's most unfortunate children; in doing so she found release from the "long loneliness", that pain of isolation that separates us through sin from the Lord and from our fellow sufferers. In a world torn by social injustice, a world which daily reaps anew the wages of sin, one finds surcease from loneliness only in the community of sinners who love one another and together worship their Creator. "We cannot love God unless we love each other, and to love we must know each other. We know him in the breaking of bread, and we know each other in the breaking of bread, and we are not alone anymore. Heaven is a banquet and life is a banquet, too, even with a crust, where there is companionship."

Dorothy Day still irritates me—for which I thank God; may he send more like her my way.

XIII

THOMAS MERTON'S

The Seven Storey Mountain

Thomas Merton became everyone's favorite monk in the 1960s and although he never graced the cover of *Time*, the media turned him into a celebrity. For Catholic liberals, Protestants and secularists he embodied the spirit of Vatican II. They loved him the more as he seemingly shook off the dogmas and outworn practices of the Church's dark age and emerged as a monk whom Americans could admire and pamper. In his writings Merton turned from the devotional works of his earlier years to address the "real" concerns of contemporary Christians. Everyone breathed easy: no more self-flagellating Trappist monasticism for Thomas Merton. He enthusiastically embraced the cause of civil rights for blacks and he became a guru to Catholic radicals who literally sat at his feet to seek his counsel on the war in Southeast Asia. Devotees of the counterculture claimed Merton as their own, for did he not share their

fascination with Eastern mysticism? Merton's refusal to abjure his monastic vows disappointed
some of his fans, but they consoled themselves
with the thought that had he not died prematurely
in 1968 he might have abandoned the monastery
and taken his rightful place in American society.
Some of his followers probably even longed to see
him find a hip girlfriend, frug in posh watering
spots and regale Johnny Carson with anecdotes of
the cloistered life. Truly here was a monk for all
seasons, one whom social activists, hippies and
"fun" people could clasp to their beaded and
denimed bosoms.

There was another Thomas Merton: Frater
Louis, the young monk who in 1948 published his
spiritual autobiography, *The Seven Storey Mountain*.
Merton later preferred to relegate this book to an
obscure place in the bibliography of his writings,
wishing as he did to obliterate the pious trium-
phalist monk who had assailed Protestants for
their heresies and spiritual fecklessness. More than
one reader has squirmed uneasily when confronted
with the hardline orthodoxy and passionate commitment to the silent life that infuse the pages of
The Seven Storey Mountain.

I once assigned the book in a college course I
taught on American thought and culture. I could
hardly contain my eagerness as we moved closer

to the day set aside to discuss the volume in class. Surely, I thought, these bright and articulate young people would be touched deeply by Merton's story of a soul's fitful journey from despair to a transcendent peace of the spirit. I bounded into class that day expecting to be greeted by effusions of thanks for assigning the book; instead: silence— a silence that by comparison made Merton's monastery sound like an Irish bar on St. Patrick's Day. The adolescent atheists in the class smirked, the Protestants frowned their disapproval and the Catholics averted their eyes and slunk down in their seats. After much threatening and cajoling I finally pried some comments from my normally voçal charges. The consensus? Thomas Merton was a bigot who had wasted his life holed up in a monastery staring at his navel.

Merton spent his first twenty-six years in circumstances many would envy. Blessed with artistically talented parents and doting maternal grandparents, who stepped in when Merton's mother and father died prematurely, young Thomas grew up in a world of cosmopolitanism and material ease. "If what most people take for granted were really true—if all you needed to be happy was to grab everything and see everything and investigate every experience and then talk about it, I should have been a very happy person, a spiritual millionaire, from the cradle even until now."

Education in France and in an English public school led to two riotous years at Cambridge University and then on to Columbia University for fraternity parties, work on student magazines, long hours of good talk with beloved friends and bachelor's and master's degrees in English literature. Ensconced in a suitably picturesque Greenwich Village apartment Merton settled down to write a doctoral dissertation, compose poetry, try his hand at fiction and review books for the *New York Times*. Here was a young man on the make, one of those brainy and aggressive young persons who fill the bookstores, bars and coffeeshops of New York City with dazzling displays of their intellectual prowess and promise.

Beneath the surface of this glitter lay a battered soul. A life of spiritual desiccation had led Merton through egoism, dissipation, flirtation with the Communist Party, despair and a sickness with life that had brought him to the brink of a nervous breakdown. Finally, God's grace penetrated the hard carapace of worldly success behind which Merton had hidden his spiritual agony. On an autumn day in 1938, unable to resist God any longer, Merton walked to the rectory of a nearby Catholic church and said to the priest: "Father, I want to become a Catholic."

The real journey—the only one that ultimately matters—began on that day. "I was about to set foot on the shore at the foot of the high, seven-circled mountain of a purgatory steeper and more arduous than I was able to imagine, and I was not at all aware of the climbing I was about to have to do." Merton could not slake his thirst with the normal believer's half-hearted attempts to serve God. A passion for totality drove him on, on into an abyss; but this time, rather than the void of nothingness, he found "love and peace, the abyss was God." The God he discovered there led him to one of those decisions that few men ever contemplate, much less make: on December 10, 1941, Thomas Merton entered the Trappist monastery of Our Lady of Gethsemani in central Kentucky. "So Brother Matthew locked the gate behind me and I was enclosed in the four walls of my new freedom."

In the years after the publication of *The Seven Storey Mountain* Merton moved beyond the traditional role of a cloistered monk. His fame as a devotional writer increased steadily in the 1950s, bringing him attention that conflicted with the anonymity of the monastic life. In the 1960s he channeled his energies into social causes and he delved deeply into the arcane mysteries of Buddhist mysticism. Merton seemed bent upon revising the monastic vocation to make it relevant to the modern world. Paradoxically, though, he implored the Father Abbot to allow him to retreat

to a hermitage on the monastery lands, a request
the long-suffering abbot acceded to several years
before Merton's death. Thomas Merton remained
a monk despite his renewed involvement with the
world. He loved the stillness of his small cinder-
block hermitage, for in the deepest reaches of his
heart lay the knowledge that God calls some men
to seek him in solitude: *"O beata solitudo."*

XIV

JOHN WOOLMAN'S

Journal

Members of the Society of Friends—more familiarly known as Quakers—present a stern test to my sense of Christian charity. Many Friends are dedicated Christians who strive to translate the Gospel imperatives into practical ways of living daily a life for and in Christ. Despite my respect for such Friends, their religion troubles me.

Arising in the seventeenth century with a fanaticism that stunned even the men of that immoderate age, the Quakers (especially in Philadelphia) gradually exchanged their fervor for commercial prosperity and a quietism that sometimes verged on self-righteousness. The much-praised asceticism—most readily observable in stark meetinghouses—that came to be a hallmark of Quakerism has often struck me as a denial of the fullness of creation. At its worst the doctrine of the Inner Light invites one to self-worship, a tendency that Chesterton scorned in *Orthodoxy*: "Of all the horrible religions the most horrible is the worship of the god within. . . . That Jones shall worship the god within him turns out ultimately to mean that Jones shall worship Jones." Most distressing of all to some Americans is the reluctance of the American Friends Service Committee to condemn murderous Communist regimes in such places as Vietnam. If the way of the Inner Light leads ineluctably in this direction, then better the world had never heard of George Fox.

Self-righteousness cuts both ways, though, and my criticism of Quakers threatens to drag me into that morass. Besides, the business of judging Quakers—as well as Catholics, Methodists, Baptists and all other Christians—belongs not to me but to God; only he knows their hearts, their secret lives and whether or not they have done his will. Then too whatever ill-feeling I harbor toward Quakerism deliquesces when confronted by the person of John Woolman, the Quaker tailor from the colonial province of West Jersey. Until his death in 1772 at the age of fifty-two, Woolman lived a life of Christian love, simplicity and self-sacrifice. The record of that life—Woolman's *Journal*—stands as one of the great Christian testimonials of the eighteenth century.

Deeply pained by the cruelty of man to man and troubled by the growing love of luxury he discerned among his fellow colonials (Quakers included), Woolman felt called of God to lead his countrymen back to the true path. He worried over his fitness to bear witness to Christ's message. How dare he, a mere humble tailor, rebuke the sinfulness he saw on every hand? Would not the proud, the rich, the socially secure laugh at this froward workman? Woolman feared the accusation of self-righteousness and he trembled at times in the presence of the mighty, but God would not allow him the ease of an untroubled conscience.

In 1743, while still a young man, Woolman undertook the first of his missions and though this one carried him only into the neighboring province of East Jersey, he had begun a life of travel for the Lord. For the next thirty years he traversed the American colonies, journeying up and down the eastern seaboard from Rhode Island to North Carolina, penetrating into the backwoods of Pennsylvania on a mission to the Indians and even venturing across the Atlantic to England. All for God, all to encourage and instruct Quaker brethren in the ways of their faith and to carry to the heathen the message of the peaceable kingdom of love, good will and gentleness. Though "of a tender constitution of body", Woolman refused to claim the excuse of a frail frame and frequent illness.

John Woolman's heart ached for all of God's suffering children, but he wept most for the black slaves who labored under the lash so that their white masters might live in comfort. The institution of slavery had yet to be isolated in the South, so Woolman could readily observe the brutality of human bondage in his native West Jersey. Worst of all, Woolman's fellow Quakers felt no qualms in participating in the enslavement of the Africans. No one protested the iniquity; no one cried out for justice. He could not bear the sight of such flagrant inhumanity. Alone at first, and then joined by others, he set out to convince Quakers of the wrongness of slavery.

The ease with which slavery sucked even the un-suspecting into its maw took on especial poignance for Woolman in 1754. In that year he settled the estate of a deceased Quaker and unthinkingly, as part of the routine duty of the executor of a will, he sold a young black boy. The memory of this deed tormented Woolman for the rest of his days and it goaded him in his efforts to combat the evil institution. Woolman prophesied that this "dark gloominess hanging over the land" would bring the wrath of God upon America if Christians continued to countenance the existence of human bondage. He, at least, would labor to stay the hand of judgment. With a patience and forebearance that could only have been a gift of God, Woolman rebuked his fellow Americans with gentle per-sistence. His tenacity finally paid off, for in 1776, four years after Woolman's death, the Quakers became the first denomination in America to bar slaveholders from membership. From that small beginning the antislavery movement would grow until a hundred years later America would at last extirpate the malignant tumor of slavery. Tragically, there were few John Woolmans—men who preached love not hate, peace not war—around in 1861; the arbitrament of the sword triumphed over Woolman's "Friendly persuasion" and the Quaker tailor's noble endeavor degenerated into a crusade of carnage.

John Woolman once called himself "a sojourner in this world"; true, but he neglected to add one word: he was *God's* sojourner. Few men have anguished more over the ravages of sin than did John Woolman and few have labored so assiduously to lighten the pall of evil that hangs over this world. Woolman followed his Lord well; through a life of renunciation and self-sacrifice he bore witness to the teachings of Jesus Christ. Like the Savior, Woolman devoted himself to the despised and forlorn, to the "least of these" whom the Lord loves so dearly.

John Woolman's sojourn came to an end on October 7, 1772; he died of smallpox in York, England, where he had gone on a mission to the English Quakers. A Quaker, yes; but above all, God's own man and a sublime Christian.

XV

CHARLES PÉGUY'S

God Speaks

In the eyes of Anglophiles I am guilty of the most egregious of betrayals. Having long ago given both heart and mind to those great English defenders of the faith, Belloc, Chesterton and Lewis, I have recently recanted. Their French Catholic contemporaries have captivated me. Georges Bernanos started it with his *Diary of a Country Priest*; then I discovered the writings of Léon Bloy, François Mauriac and Paul Claudel; Charles Péguy has completed the alienation of my affections.

Born in Orléans in 1874, Péguy came of peasant stock. His widowed mother, who mended chairs to furnish a livelihood for her son and her elderly mother, raised Péguy in an atmosphere of stubborn peasant tenacity and regular—if somewhat perfunctory—Catholic observance. As a *lycée* student Péguy forsook the Church for republicanism and socialism. In the 1890s he came to Paris, that magnet for aspiring French intellectuals in all ages, to prepare for a career as a university professor. The scintillation and robust spirits of the French Left enthralled the young man from the provinces; he leaped into the fray of workers' strikes and student protests and in 1898 he led the student brigades into the streets of Paris to rage at the persecution of Captain Alfred Dreyfus. In 1900—having failed his comprehensive examinations at the École Normale—he launched the *Cahiers de la Quinzaine*, a journal in which to propagate his own ideas and those of his friends. Between 1900 and 1914 Péguy shaped the *Cahiers* into one of the most provocative features of French intellectual life in the prewar years. When the guns of August thundered in 1914 Péguy shouldered arms in defense of his beloved France. He died on September 5, 1914, one of the first casualties of the battle of the Marne.

One salient biographical detail must be added: in 1908 Péguy returned to the Church with the simple declaration to a friend that "I have got back my faith. I am a Catholic." No peace came to him. His wife—heir to a family tradition of militant agnosticism—refused to have their marriage blessed by the Church or to allow their three children to be baptized. Prevented from taking Communion by Madame Péguy's adamantine *No!* Péguy stayed away from the Mass altogether. Full fellowship

with the body of believers would not have solved
his problems anyway, for he found himself at
odds with many of his fellow Catholics. He sniped
at the clergy and chastized the Church for allying
herself with the bourgeoisie. His continuing devotion to republicanism and socialism—albeit a
socialism according to St. Francis rather than Karl
Marx—ill-befitted him to move easily among the
Church's staunchest defenders in France. As a
Pascalian man of the heart, Péguy disliked the
Thomistic revival then flourishing under the hand
of such Catholic thinkers as the young Jacques
Maritain. Péguy's devotion to the metaphysics
of Henri Bergson nearly got his own writings
placed on the Index. Péguy returned to the faith
of his childhood, but he would be his own Catholic; as Emmanuel Mounier, the philosopher of
Personalism, once said: "Péguy is a man who
cannot be annexed."

Although Péguy defies the pigeonholers, at
least one label suits him perfectly: he belongs
to that small company of truly distinguished
Christian writers of our century. To discover this
for oneself is no easy task, for most of his works
are hard to come by in America, either because
they have not been translated into English or once
translated, they have failed to remain in print.
To my thinking the reader in pursuit of Charles

Péguy should scour libraries and ransack second-hand bookstores in search of *God Speaks*, a selection of Péguy's poetry taken from the *Cahiers* of 1910 to 1912.

As the title indicates, Péguy had the audacity to put words into the mouth of God, to turn God into a monologist who comments on the foibles and frailties of his creatures with a mixture of amusement, exasperation, anger and tenderness. This risky endeavor invites everything from banality to blasphemy, but in Péguy's hands this rhetorical device works splendidly. Take, for example, a passage in the section entitled "Innocence and Experience". Here Péguy ventures into a realm where few Christians dare to enter: he portrays a God of laughter who delights in the antics of his children. Péguy's God chuckles as he watches a small boy drifting off to sleep while saying his prayers, the Paternosters entangling themselves with the Ave Marias in a drowsy devotional. Surely an affront to the majesty of God! God remarks:

> I have never seen anything so funny and I therefore
>   know of nothing so beautiful in the world
> As that child going to sleep as he says his prayers.

Péguy's God can as easily express sorrow, the pain with which he watched as his own creatures crucified his Only Begotten Son, Jesus Christ.

How could mere mortals ever hope to understand the mystery of divine anguish? Péguy succeeds with a simplicity at once startling and profound:

> Now every man has the right to bury his son,
> Every man on earth, if he has had that great misfortune
> Not to have died before his son. And I alone, I, God,
> Arms tied by that adventure,
> I alone, at the moment, father after so many fathers,
> I alone could not bury my son.

Anger and impatience at times mark God's voice as he observes this being Man, the product of God's own handiwork. These beloved creatures oftentimes seem incapable of little more than of indulging in gross injustices toward one another, of wallowing in sties of immorality and of mocking the very God who made them. Infuriated by this treachery, Péguy's God vows to mete out divine retribution upon these vile and petty ingrates. But a twinkle appears in God's eye, for he knows how little he—the Creator, the mighty Lord of Hosts—can resist the supplications of penitent sinners.

> How do you expect me to defend myself? My son told them everything. And not only did he do that. But he put himself at their head. And they are like a great fleet of yore, like an innumerable fleet attacking the great king.

Charles Péguy lived a life too short, too wracked with the trials and frustrations of this world. But his death did not leave us empty-handed. He gave us a gift of immeasurable worth: Péguy's poetry stands as a monument to a God who speaks and to fallen man's ability to hear the Master's voice.

XVI

REINHOLD NIEBUHR'S

*Leaves from the Notebook
of a Tamed Cynic*

Reinhold Niebuhr often walked a lonely road. He rarely pleased anyone all the time and he offended many people most of the time. His love of the dialectic, with its paradoxes and apparent contradictions that dissolve into higher truths, prevented less agile minds from following him. He infuriated liberal Protestants by assailing their naiveté and by exposing the groundlessness of their optimism. Fundamentalists attacked him as a destroyer of the eternal verities because he rejected biblical literalism and called for unrelenting war against social injustice. Secular reformers found Niebuhr a strange ally; in the midst of their most grandiloquent hymns to the future Niebuhr would insist on stopping the music to remind them of the worm of sin in the apple of utopia. Strange fellow, this Niebuhr; but none would deny that he was his own man.

Niebuhr was not always *the* Reinhold Niebuhr;

he too apprenticed in obscurity: the years from 1915 to 1928 when he pastored the Bethel Evangelical Church in Detroit. As a young man of twenty-three, fresh from Eden Theological Seminary in St. Louis and two years of study at Yale, Niebuhr left the secure precincts of academe to assume the yoke of pastoral work. His real education began on the first Sunday morning he stepped into the pulpit in Detroit. *Leaves from the Notebook of a Tamed Cynic* chronicles the quotidian realities of that education.

With all due respect to Pastor Niebuhr, I must confess that I have never much liked men of the cloth. In my boyhood two types of Protestant preachers shaped my image of the clergy. None irritated me quite so much as that unctuous, Bible-toting breed, long on piety and short on brains, who in orotund tones rendered the Gospel about as exciting as a croquet game. A second type did equal damage; he *thumped* his Bible and tried to frighten me into heaven with vivid descriptions of the everlasting fires of hell. To his credit he at least entertained me. During my college years I discovered the liberal clergyman, this one long on brains (or at least possessed of a patina of intellectualism) and short on piety; never did the words "sin" or "divine sacrifice" escape his lips, for he had dedicated his ministry to the proposition that salvation comes through sociology, psychology and the left wing of the Democratic Party. In my disgust I looked to the Roman Catholic clergy, certain that here I would find more admirable servants of God; instead I stumbled across hip young priests who desecrated the Mass by allowing adolescents to plunk guitars and praise God with renditions of insipid Simon and Garfunkel songs.

One hates to give up stereotypes; they make life so much simpler. In *Leaves from the Notebook of a Tamed Cynic* Reinhold Niebuhr shattered some of mine, for he forced me to see the minister as a flesh-and-blood human being beset with all the problems that our humanity brings to us and, in addition, burdened with the awesome responsibility of shepherding an often petty and quarrelsome flock of church members who expect their pastor to be an infallible blend of spiritual guide, administrator, fund-raiser, psychologist and entertainer; in his spare time he should work toward acquiring his badge of sainthood. The wonder lies not in the minister's failure to measure up to these standards but in his willingness to accept the challenge at all.

Niebuhr's tears and laughter mingle as he recounts the early years of his pastorate. He immediately realized that "there is something ludicrous about a callow young fool like myself standing up to preach a sermon to these good folks." Who could not love that same callow fool when he asks plaintively: "Where did anyone ever learn in a seminary how to conduct or help with a Ladies Aid meeting?" His decision to visit all his parishioners in their homes led to agonizing attacks of shyness; back and forth he would pace on the sidewalk, steeling his courage to face these people on their own grounds. The frustrations of comforting the sick and dying bedeviled him: "This sickness of Miss Z's is getting on my nerves. I can't think of anything for the rest of the day after coming from that bed of pain." He struggled on, knowing that his church members depended upon him for strength, hope and solace; he alone knew how frail were the young pastor's shoulders.

Despite the heavy burden of ministering to his parishioners Pastor Niebuhr increasingly turned his attention to the larger society of which his church formed but a part. Detroit furnished a fitting scene for one concerned with the social ethics of Christianity; its booming industrial life, presided over by the genius of mass production, Henry Ford, made Detroit a modern American city *par excellence*. This new industrial order distressed Niebuhr. The dull monotony of the assembly line turned men into automatons; long lay-offs brought hard times to those dependent upon regular paychecks; and worst of all, mass industrial society bred impersonality, callousness and spiritual malaise. Niebuhr could have averted his eyes and moved serenely through the middle-class world of his parishioners, but his troubled conscience would not rest. In sermons, at conferences and in magazine articles Niebuhr began to explore the ethical import of the Gospel.

Niebuhr came dangerously close at times in the 1920s to forgetting that all schemes for social betterment must be founded upon the irreducibility of the individual sinner. Yet he never fell prey to the impatience and overbearing self-righteousness that so often characterized social gospelers of the time. He understood that a people schooled for centuries in the ethics of Protestant individualism could not be won overnight to the demands of a broader social ethic. He reminded himself: "Nor have you a right to insinuate that they [middle-class church members] are all hypocrites just because they don't see what you see." Niebuhr repudiated the "sophomoric cocksureness" displayed by many of his liberal colleagues during the 1920s.

By 1928 Reinhold Niebuhr had garnered considerable attention in Protestant circles; his articles in national magazines, his activities in behalf of social action and his steady round of speaking engagements at colleges and universities had lifted him from the obscurity of Bethel Church's pulpit. Union Theological Seminary, recognizing a rising star, invited Niebuhr to assume the position of Professor of Applied Christianity. Niebuhr bade his congregation farewell in 1928, but not without regret: those thirteen years had been ones of deepening understanding of the meaning of the Gospel in the lives of ordinary men and women. At Bethel Church—as Niebuhr wrote almost thirty years later—he had led the simple life of a pastor, "meeting human problems on all levels of weal and woe, and trying to be helpful in fashioning a 'community of grace'. . . ."

XVII

MALCOLM MUGGERIDGE'S

Something Beautiful for God

Despair tracks me through this world; it lurks in the shadows, biding its time, waiting to slip its greedy fingers around my heart. Despair has many allies; their strength overwhelms one at times and one searches futilely for the presence of God in this torn and sorrowful world. Fierce nihilistic ideologies roam the land. Wars and ceaseless violence drench the earth with blood. Suffering that defies description rages in every corner of the planet: starvation drags small children through an agonizing dance of death and horrible diseases maim and destroy. Malice, hatred, greed and lust slink from their hiding places and walk openly to the applause of their votaries. In America 1.5 million unborn children died in 1980, tiny lives snuffed out for the sake of women's rights. If God does not exist, then surely Satan does.

Two thousand years ago in the land of Palestine a mob howled its rage and a detachment of Roman soldiers nailed a young Jew to a wooden cross.

That cruel fact paradoxically brought hope to mankind. God sent his Only Begotten Son, Jesus Christ, to redeem a vile brood of sinners. Hope triumphed over despair. Two thousand years is a long time and man possesses a short memory. He needs to be reminded of the promise and possibility symbolized by the Cross that loomed out of the gathering gloom on Golgotha: hope, not despair; love, not hatred; salvation, not nothingness.

Halfway round the globe amidst the heart-breaking misery of what novelist V. S. Naipaul has called "that cruel city", Calcutta, India, a small woman reminds one of the meaning of the Cross. Mother Teresa gently picks a tiny infant from a refuse heap and hope vanquishes despair; she bathes the ghastly wounds of a leper and love triumphs over hatred; she cradles the head of a dying beggar and Jesus Christ lives in this world. "Love", she says, "is a fruit in season at all times, and within reach of every hand. Anyone may gather it and no limit is set." God has not forsaken us, for only God could give a Mother Teresa to an undeserving race of sinners.

In *Something Beautiful for God*, Malcolm Muggeridge, the gadfly of British journalism for the past fifty years, records his brief but poignant contact with Mother Teresa. Having interviewed her in London for BBC television, Muggeridge sought Mother Teresa's permission to film her and her Missionaries of Charity at their work in Calcutta. Reluctantly she agreed, but once having consented, she wrote to Muggeridge: "Now let us do something beautiful for God." In 1969, accompanied by a film and sound crew, Muggeridge flew to India.

Throughout his long life Muggeridge has looked with a hard and practiced eye upon the follies of his fellow men. From the Soviet workers' paradise of the 1930s to the latest utopian fantasies of leftist reformers, he has chronicled and pilloried self-serving protestations of benevolence and good will. Anyone who has read his devastating assaults on Sidney and Beatrice Webb knows what his slashing sarcasm and mordant wit can do to weak-minded, sentimental humanitarians. Confronted daily with the idiocies of this world, Muggeridge might easily have become the classic type of jaded, cynical journalist, cackling at the yahoos as he records their antics—a British H. L. Mencken perhaps. Might have, for Christianity spared Muggeridge that fate. His conversion softened his wrath, but he remained unimpressed with those who prate of their love for their fellow men; as Muggeridge knows, talk is cheap.

In Mother Teresa, Muggeridge found the true and pure goodness he had fruitlessly sought in his encounters with self-appointed lovers of humanity. As he watched her move among the outcasts of Indian society, as he walked with her through the slums of Calcutta, he realized that he stood in the presence of one touched by the hand of God. "It will be for posterity to decide whether she is a saint", he writes. "I only say of her that in a dark time she is a burning and shining light; in a cruel time, a living embodiment of Christ's gospel of love; in a godless time, the Word dwelling among us, full of grace and truth. For this, all who have the inestimable privilege of knowing her, or knowing of her, must be eternally grateful."

Two especially of the many photographs in *Something Beautiful for God* graphically illustrate Muggeridge's graceful words. In one of these Mother Teresa hugs a tiny child to her bosom. Her hands—strong hands that have earned their wrinkles through hard labor—cradle the child. Mother Teresa's face—a sublimely beautiful face when measured by God's own standards—bears a deep sadness, a sadness that springs from an unblinking knowledge of the suffering of humankind. But her face also radiates a love and compassion rooted in the realization that Christ dwells in this sickly and malnourished child.

The other photograph captures Mother Teresa in another mood, for here a marvelously beatific smile wreathes her face. She has lived for decades amidst suffering so great that one might curse God for allowing it to exist. Yet she smiles with a radiance that draws its energy from her love of God. Muggeridge writes of Mother Teresa and her co-workers: "I have never met such delightful, happy women, or such an atmosphere of joy as they create."

The distance from my despair to Mother Teresa's joy surpasses the thousands of miles that separate the United States from India. I am shamed by that thought, shamed because a small Albanian nun has discovered the meaning of the Cross while I have not. Mother Teresa knows no despair, for her love of God and her selfless devotion to his children have banished it from her world. From now on when the abyss beckons me I shall open Muggeridge's book to those two photographs of Mother Teresa and let her luminous beauty remind me of the power of love to illuminate the darkest of nights.

XVIII

EVELYN WAUGH'S

Edmund Campion: Jesuit and Martyr

The great days of England have passed; a nation
that once bestrode the world has been reduced
to a footnote in the chronicle of our times. The
legacy of her glorious days remains, however.
So long as Western civilization survives men will
remember the dazzling brilliance of the Elizabethan
era, that half century in which an England fired by
ebullient optimism stamped her indelible imprint
upon the West. During her reign from 1558 to
1603, Elizabeth Tudor propelled England to the
forefront of international influence. She brought a
measure of order out of the religious turmoil that
had plagued Englishmen since her father, King
Henry VIII, had severed ties with Rome in the
1530s. Her bold seamen ranged across the Atlantic
and the voyages of such swashbucklers as Sir
Humphrey Gilbert and Sir Walter Raleigh set
the stage for permanent English settlement in the
New World. Poets and playwrights—most notably
Shakespeare—won acclaim for England in the realm

of letters. The accomplishments and prospects of their beloved motherland swelled the hearts of Englishmen.

English Roman Catholics can be forgiven if they do not join their countrymen in hymning the praises of Good Queen Bess. Their delight in the magnificence of that reign must always be mitigated by one stark and terrible fact: Elizabeth subjected Roman Catholics to a brutal persecution. For their loyalty to the historic faith of their fathers these men and women bore the brunt of Elizabeth's notorious fury; hatred, civil disability, staggering fines, imprisonment and death awaited those who paid allegiance to the pope. Elizabeth especially singled out the Roman priests for persecution, for if they could be exterminated then surely Roman Catholicism would wither. Rome would not forsake the beleaguered flock; as priest after priest mounted the scaffold eager volunteers slipped across the English Channel to take up the Church's standard.

Evelyn Waugh—novelist, Englishman and convert to Roman Catholicism—offers the story of one such priest in *Edmund Campion: Jesuit and Martyr*. When Queen Elizabeth paid her first royal visit to Oxford University in 1566, a young man of twenty-six caught her eye. Edmund Campion, Fellow of St. John's College, dazzled the Queen and her courtiers with his eloquence and sparkling erudition. Both Sir William Cecil and the Earl of Leicester marked him as one with a brilliant future in the Church of England, and Leicester quickly extended his patronage to the young scholar.

Campion threw away his future; a year's intensive study of the Church Fathers convinced him that Roman Catholicism alone preserved the true faith. The seductive voice of power and preferment urged him to hold his tongue, to compromise his beliefs for the sake of his career. Why sacrifice advancement to a few quibbling points of theology? Campion's stubborn *No!* sealed his fate: in 1572 the Crown outlawed him and he fled to the Spanish Netherlands. A year later he joined the Society of Jesus and went to Prague in Bohemia to teach in a Jesuit-run school. In 1580 he cast his lot with his persecuted countrymen and returned to England; the fair-haired youth of promise now became a hated and hunted fugitive.

Campion bore no malice toward the Queen; his mission involved no seditious effort to overthrow the kingdoms of this world. As he wrote soon after returning to his native land, he had come "to preach the Gospel, to minister the sacraments, to instruct the simple, to reform sinners, to confute errors." Campion knew that the gibbet awaited him, but he would pay that price in full in order to comfort his Roman Catholic countrymen and to rally them to withstand persecution. "The expense is reckoned, the enterprise is begun; it is of God, it cannot be withstood. So the faith was planted; so it must be restored."

For over a year Campion eluded the agents of the Crown as he passed from town to town, saying the Mass, hearing confessions and succoring the Church's despised followers. The net gradually closed upon the priest who had become a hero to English Roman Catholics. In July of 1581 one George Eliot, a professional priest-hunter posing as a Catholic, betrayed Campion. Campion's captors paraded their catch through the streets of London for the edification of the mob; "CAMPION THE SEDITIOUS JESUIT" (as the sign attached to him read) had been brought to earth. The Queen ordered the prisoner before her, and here for the first time in ten years Campion came face to face with his old patron Leicester. With the Queen's approval, Leicester offered a pardon to Campion if he would publicly renounce his faith and enter the ministry of the Church of England. The path to fame and power would be opened to him again. Leicester had misjudged his man: to his amazement his former protégé refused the bargain. Leicester and the Queen could understand why a man would risk death to seize power, but, as Waugh writes, "to die deliberately, without hope of release, for an idea, was something beyond their comprehension."

In late November of 1581, after several months
of torture on the rack, Campion, accompanied by
several other priests, came to trial. Campion's
body was broken, but his spirit remained indom-
itable and his faith firm. That Campion should
die had been decided when he had refused to
recant; the formal trial intended only to preserve
the façade of justice and to expose Campion and
his fellow priests as plotters against the Queen.
Campion turned the proceedings to his own
purpose; he swore his allegiance to the Queen and
hammered home the point—in a disconcertingly
effective way—that his "guilt" arose not from treason but from his refusal to abjure his faith. Campion
hurled defiance at his judges: "In condemning us
you condemn all your own ancestors—all the
ancient priests, bishops and kings—all that was
once the glory of England, the island of saints, and
the most devoted child of the See of Peter. . . . To
be condemned with these lights—not of England
only, but of the world—by their degenerate de-
scendants, is both gladness and glory to us."

"Guilty of treason", the court replied.

In the biting cold of a December day Campion—
the "seditious Jesuit"—mounted the scaffold at
Tyburn. A large crowd had gathered for the
execution; some were Roman Catholics who
wept for the beloved Father Campion, but most of
the spectators had come to enjoy the show. To this

crowd Campion proclaimed his faith one last time: "I am a Catholic man and a priest; in that faith have I lived and in that faith I intend to die." Edmund Campion dropped to his death and his short life of forty-one years came to an end. Some of the bystanders probably muttered that Campion had foolishly squandered his talents to die an abject and meaningless death. If his death held no meaning, English Catholics failed to grasp that fact, for the name of Edmund Campion would long remain on their lips, steeling their courage and inspiring them to cling tenaciously to the faith of their fathers. For them Father Campion's life and death were—in Waugh's words—a "simple story of heroism and holiness". The blood of a martyr had once again triumphed over the principalities and powers of this earth.

XIX

C. S. LEWIS'

Surprised by Joy

In a song entitled "Heaven Help the Child" Mickey Newbury, one of the best country songwriters since Hank Williams, says that life "can offer plenty to a young man with a vision, so they say."[2] With or without a vision, young or old, life does offer plenty. The beauty and bounty of this world seem at times to answer one's every need. Even without delving into the considerable (if ephemeral) pleasures of sin for a season, one can find—with a modicum of good fortune—a life replete with happiness. A house bursting with creature comforts, satisfying and challenging work, the love of a good mate, the devotion of one's children—all this lies within one's grasp. What more could one ask?

The gnawing suspicion that something is missing will not go away. An inkling of that indefinable

[2] "Heaven Help the Child" by Mickey Newbury. Copyright 1972 by Acuff-Rose Publications, Inc. Used by permission of the publisher. All rights reserved.

something comes to one in its own time and way: through the lilt of a poem by Yeats, in the sudden lambency of the sunlight that dances across a pool of still water, in the aching beauty of a Chopin nocturne. To say that these bring pleasure stops short of the mark, for they provoke something deeper: an intense desire and longing, a wanting that reduces the normal cravings of human beings to triviality. Longing for what? Usually we do not know, for we are faced with the ineffable, the inexpressible, the realm of evanescent substances. We do know one thing for certain: despite the pain in our hearts we would not forgo this stab of desire.

C. S. Lewis called this phenomenon "Joy". "The stab, the pang, the inconsolable longing" first struck Lewis in his childhood, and it recurred throughout his early life until it led him to the grand culmination, to that moment when the inconsolable longing found the object of its desire in Jesus Christ. Lewis followed a tortuous path to reach this destination; the outcome remained in doubt for a long time as the world, the flesh and the devil unleashed their practiced wiles upon Lewis. The "Pagan"—as Lewis calls himself—was susceptible to these blandishments; God found a recalcitrant soul in the young C. S. Lewis.

A boyhood bout with the fears and rigors of hardshell religion left Lewis inured to Christianity and glad to be rid of the bothersome demands of the faith. While still a schoolboy he "formed the opinion that the universe was, in the main, a rather regrettable institution." Through his early teen-aged years he nurtured a cosmic pessimism, dabbled in "occultist fancies" and, under the tutelage of one "Pogo", a young school master and "man about town", Lewis, a self-described fourteen-year-old lout, "began to labor very hard to make myself into a fop, a cad, and a snob." Only divine insight could have spied the future Christian in such unpromising material.

The lout began to lust and though he sampled the delights of the flesh, he soon discovered that sex led only to emptiness. More importantly, Lewis happened upon Wagnerian opera, Nordic mythology and the pantheon of heroic Norse gods. Good atheist that he was by now, he did not believe in the actual existence of these gods, but the tales borne out of the far north country sent him into ecstasy. Lewis gave himself to "something very like adoration, some kind of disinterested self-abandonment to an object which securely claimed this by simply being the object it was." Could this be the sought-after object of desire? No, but though attached to the Norse gods, Lewis' "worshipfulness" attained a level never reached by those Christians for whom God exists mainly to fulfil their every need. Lewis,

by contrast, could adore gods who refused man's
quid pro quo.

After miserable stints at a number of schools,
Lewis embarked on two years of private study
with a Mr. Kirkpatrick, a retired teacher and old
friend of Lewis' father. The "Great Knock",
as he called Kirkpatrick, schooled Lewis in a
rigorous rationalism that confirmed the youth in
his already well-developed atheism. Kirkpatrick's
tutoring paid off: Lewis won his scholarship to
Oxford and in the summer of 1917 he went up to
Trinity College to begin his studies. The young
man who walked the emerald lawns of Oxford
that summer had arrived at an uneasy dualism in
his thinking. "On the one side a many-islanded
sea of poetry and myth; on the other a glib and
shallow 'rationalism'. Nearly all that I loved I
believed to be imaginary; nearly all that I believed
to be real I thought grim and meaningless."

After service on the Western Front with the
Somerset Light Infantry, Lewis returned to Oxford to begin the journey that would lead to his
conversion to Christianity. He experienced no
epiphanies along the way, no thunderous voices
from heaven, no emotional upheavals. He quickly
jettisoned his atheism for a then-popular brand
of philosophical Idealism. From a belief in the
Absolute posited by Idealists he progressed to
theism, and from this doctrine he finally reached

the welcoming arms of God. Lewis' search hardly constituted the anguished quest of a lost soul, however, for he resisted any such seeking after God. "To me, as I then was, they might as well have talked about the mouse's search for the cat." But the mouse found the cat: on a night in 1929 Lewis "gave in, and admitted that God was God, knelt and prayed: perhaps that night, the most dejected and reluctant convert in all England."

God now existed for Lewis and that God was a Divine Person, but the new convert had still not accepted the Incarnation. Lewis could not hold out much longer, though, and he soon adopted Christianity in its entirety. "I knew very well when, but hardly how, the final step was taken. I was driven to Whipsnade one sunny morning. When we set out I did not believe that Jesus Christ is the Son of God, and when we reached the zoo I did."

And Joy? Lewis for the first time discerned its true meaning. Throughout his life that delicious pang of desire had been leading him to this moment. By a circuitous route filled with tricks and snares God had lured Lewis to the great "surprise". "But I now know that the experience, considered as a state of my own mind, had never had the kind of importance I once gave it. It was valuable only as a pointer to something other and outer. While that other was in doubt, the pointer naturally loomed large in my thoughts." C. S. Lewis had found the right direction; he had turned homeward at last, "surprised by Joy" and bound for glory.

XX

The Autobiography of St. Ignatius Loyola

As a young boy growing up in the sheltered world of Protestant fundamentalism I felt a shiver run up my spine whenever I heard the word "Jesuit". I feared all Roman Catholics—though I had never knowingly seen one in the flesh—but I experienced a special revulsion at the mention of those sinister Jesuits. From anti-Catholic tracts and from the fiery sermons of fundamentalist preachers I shaped an image of the Jesuit. He was a wily and cunning figure who lurked in the shadows cast by an iniquitous and oppressive Church. He prowled the corridors of power, whispering in the ears of kings and ministers of state. He twisted the truth—even lied boldly—to further the ends of Romish domination. He crouched at the foot of the papal throne awaiting his master's bidding. Worst of all, I suspected that the Jesuit snatched up small boys to immure them behind the impregnable walls of the Church until their minds could be bent to the service of the Scarlet Woman of Revelation.

A small (very small) kernel of truth lay within my phantasmagorical image of the Jesuits. Since its founding in 1540 the Society of Jesus has furnished the shock troops of the papacy. The Jesuits challenged Protestant heretics, tangled with infidels, founded universities, planted the banner of the Church in the remote reaches of the Americas and carried the message of Christ the King to the distant lands of the East. They suffered death by fire and sword, felt the sting of the lash and bore the privations of hunger and thirst. Had the pope commanded, they would have stormed the gates of hell itself, and no doubt would have caused Satan more than a bit of trepidation in the process. Noble men, these: champions of the faith, unflaggingly devoted to the Church.

It began with one man—Ignatius of Loyola—a Basque soldier who in 1521 exchanged his sword and armor for sackcloth and a pilgrim's staff. In 1553, knowing that he hadn't many years left, Ignatius felt the urge to set down the story of his conversion and of the years of struggle that had culminated in the founding of the Society of Jesus. His health failing and his days cumbered with the burdens of administration, Ignatius snatched moments from his tiring duties as General of the order to recount to Father Luis González de Cámara the events of his earlier life. González rushed from each session to jot down the words of his leader; from these notes came *The Auto-biography of St. Ignatius Loyola*—the story of *El Peregrino*, the pilgrim.

God often finds his saints in the unlikeliest of places and circumstances. Who of Ignatius' early companions would have guessed the mission that lay in store for him? The opening words of the *Autobiography* indicate no preparation for sainthood: "Until the age of twenty-six he was a man given over to vanities of the world; with a great and vain desire to win fame he delighted especially in the exercise of arms." The high romance of the Spanish soul speaks through these lines, for Ignatius, filled with the vitality of youth and fired with visions of a dashing career at arms, had begun to make his mark as a warrior. But the god of battles disregards youthful dreams when he deals the cards of fate: in May of 1521, while defending the citadel of Pamplona against French attack, Ignatius suffered a severe leg wound. His quest for fame and glory would have to await the verdict of a long convalescence.

Ignatius must have cursed his lot more than once in the long months that followed. Incapacitated and confined to his pallet Ignatius saw his dreams begin to evanesce. He called for books to while away the tedious hours; at least he could refire his imagination in the pages of chivalrous romances.

None of these "worldly and fictitious books" could be found (or so his attendants said); Ignatius groaned at the volumes proffered him: a life of Christ and a collection of saints' lives. Unexpectedly he liked what he read, but when he laid aside these pious books thoughts of chivalrous deeds and alluring women streamed back into his mind. "Nevertheless, Our Lord assisted him, causing other thoughts that arose from the things he read to follow these."

Gradually the example of St. Francis and St. Dominic took hold of Ignatius; what mattered worldly fame if one could be as these saints? A vision confirmed Ignatius in his newly found inspiration; one night as he lay awake Our Lady and the Christ Child appeared to him. "From this sight he received for a considerable time very great consolation, and he was left with such loathing for his whole past life and especially for things of the flesh, that it seemed that all the fantasies he had previously pictured in his mind were driven from it." Ignatius had taken the first step on the path to sainthood.

That journey would not be an easy one; the sword rests far more easily in a man's hand than does the Cross upon his back. Beset with remorse for his sins, Ignatius undertook an arduous course of penance. His ignorance compelled him to return to school to learn his Latin alongside schoolboys. Some of his countrymen sniffed the acrid odor of heresy in Ignatius' growing fervor and in his talk of visions. Their suspicion was understandable, for all Europe—the Europe of the true faith—threatened to be engulfed by the waves of rebellion sweeping out of England, the German states and Switzerland. Just to be safe, agents of the Spanish Inquisition questioned Ignatius and kept a close eye on his spiritual progress. Despite these humiliations and setbacks Ignatius and the small band of followers that had gathered about him would not be dissuaded. In 1538 they trekked to Rome to seek papal blessing for their venture. In 1540 Pope Paul III, the pontiff who would at last shake the Church from its torpor and corruption, gave official recognition to the Society of Jesus.

Ignatius became the *propositus* or General of the new order, a position he held until his death in 1556. From suspicions of heresy Ignatius and his holy soldiers quickly moved to the forefront of the spiritual renewal that the Church undertook in the middle of the sixteenth century. Ignatius and his Jesuits played no small part in checking the spread of Protestantism; as much as anyone he helped to infuse Roman Catholicism with a new energy and vigor.

God chose well when he placed his mark upon a young Basque knight filled with dreams of worldly fame. Spain lost a good soldier, but the

Church gained a saint. Once again the grace of God moved in its mysterious way, foiling the plans of men and revealing the Divine Presence that suffuses the mundane events of our small lives.

XXI

LÉON BLOY'S

The Woman Who Was Poor

The words vary according to time, place and preacher, but the message remains the same: "A Christian should not be a gloom merchant, moping through life with his chin on his chest. He should be happy, filled with joy because he knows that his Redeemer liveth." Not bad advice in its own way, for this world belongs to God; he sent his Son to redeem it and he has promised eternal life to those who follow him. Who can imagine a greater invitation to happiness? Perhaps the Christian can be forgiven for sailing blithely through life, shouting to all who will hear: "Rejoice! Christ reigns and all is well."

If this be true, then what does one make of the French novelist Léon Bloy? The man certainly appears to have been a Christian, or at least his books burn with the passion of a man obsessed with the Gospel. Yet he picked at his despair like a dog gnawing on a scab. To his fiancée, Jeanne, he wrote on November 21, 1889: "In spite of the strong attraction that the vague idea of happiness has for me, my most powerful nature always inclines me toward unhappiness, toward sorrow, and even toward despair." Bloy would not relent; of his masterpiece *The Woman Who Was Poor* (1897), he wrote: ". . . For it is itself a long digression on the evil of living, the infernal misfortune of existence, hogs lacking any snout with which to root for titbits, in a society without God."

Clotilde Maréchale—the woman of the title—lives a wretched existence; at the age of thirty she has known only "poverty, cruelty, despair". She shares a verminous flat with her wheedling mother and her mother's lover, Chapuis, a drunken old man who once tried to rape Clotilde. Pélopidas Gacougnol, a painter, rescues her from this degradation, and his kindness—which asks nothing in return—gives her the first happiness of her life. Her natural beauty and intelligence emerge from the rags and filth of poverty as she becomes part of a circle comprised of Gacougnol and his friends, Léopold, an illuminator of manuscripts, and the writer Cain Marchenoir. Clotilde knows this bliss cannot last; her suffering has retreated not fled. Her brief idyll ends when Chapuis murders Gacougnol and the gossiping tongues of Paris turn the innocent Clotilde into the scarlet woman of the painter's undoing. She marries Léopold and bears him a son. They live happily for a time,

secure in the routines of domesticity and joyful
in their love of God. Impending blindness forces
Léopold to forsake his craft; they slide into the maw
of poverty and the infant Lazare dies of an illness
brought on by the vileness of their surroundings.
Their beloved Marchenoir dies and Léopold soon
follows him to the grave. Clotilde gives her re-
maining possessions to the poor and becomes a
mendicant, dragging herself through the streets of
Paris, an old woman at the age of forty-eight.

Bloy's preoccupation with degradation, suffering
and poverty might tempt one to lump him with
his contemporary Émile Zola, who in such novels
as *Thérèse Raquin* probed the underside of Parisian
life with a perverse fascination. This would be to
ignore Bloy's Roman Catholicism, a passionate—
even violent—devotion that compelled him to
wrest transcendent meaning from man's losing
battle with life. For Bloy, man wanders the earth
disconsolately, an exile from the Edenic paradise
of his innocence. In body and soul he bears the
pain of this separation. To be human is to suffer
the hurt for which no anodyne exists in this life.
"For the human soul is a gong of pain, on which
the slightest percussion sets up vibrations that
continually grow, waves that spread outwards in
limitless circles of dread. . . ."

With his vituperative brilliance Bloy savaged
those who attempted to shelter themselves from

suffering, whether with money, social position or
with that great curse of the bourgeoisie everywhere,
respectability. Bloy would have no compromise
on this point; for him men of means existed solely to
give to the poor and thus perhaps to ransom their
own souls from the flames of hell. As Clotilde,
an old woman in rags, wanders the streets of
Paris, "those comfortable, well-dressed Christians"
avert their eyes, shocked by such an affront to
propriety and good taste. Surely this woman must
be mad, they mutter, as they hurry on to the
theater and to dinner in a luxurious restaurant.
Bloy lashes out at these pious hypocrites who
would have rejected Christ for violating the
accepted canons. The poor of Paris, those who
have no money or respectability to blind their eyes
to the divine light, hold Clotilde in awe: "and in
the churches there are a few women of the poor
who consider her a saint."

Clotilde discovers what for Bloy is a truth so
frightening that only a bare handful of Christians
can confront it unblinkingly. "By dint of suffering, this woman, a living and strong, courageous
Christian, has learned that there is only one way of
making contact with God, and that this way, for a
woman especially, is Poverty." Make no mistake:
Bloy means exactly what he says. Is it true? How
easy to give quick and glib assent; after all, Christ
loved the poor especially and the Roman Catholic

Church has always exalted those who forsake material goods for the love of God and fellow man. But think again: what about those of us who are not poor, who to some extent partake of the abundance of this world? Does Bloy mean to bar us from paradise? Or do we bar ourselves because we allow our possessions to distract us from what God would have us do? Anyone who has pondered this question even slightly cannot but be left disquieted. What if Bloy is right?

Léon Bloy scandalized the Christians of his time. He was too intense, too serious—and, perhaps, too Christian—for their tastes. He despised mediocrity, and all around him—especially among his fellow believers—he saw that which he hated most. Like the prophets of the Old Testament he stormed and raged at God's people for their betrayal of their Lord. Bloy's obsessiveness offended those who wanted a Christianity of convenience, a faith that would give them this world and heaven too. What an appalling work *The Woman Who Was Poor* must have been to these people. Most appalling of all to mediocre Christians—both then and now—are Clotilde's final words: "*There is only one misery and that is—NOT TO BE SAINTS.*"

XXII

T. S. ELIOT'S

Murder in the Cathedral

The complexity of this world almost overwhelms one at times. Shades of gray confront us when we long desperately to choose between black and white. We spin through life in a dance of confusion, grasping for simple answers and finding only more difficult questions. Perhaps death is the great simplifier, the resolution of our complexities. Yet to ponder the meaning of death simply raises more unanswerable questions. How satisfying, then, to consider the death of a Christian martyr. To die for the faith, to meet death nobly with the name of God on one's lips, to be liberated from sorrow and to stand before the throne of God—yes, that is the answer, that is the act that unsnarls life's tangled skein. Is there a subtle temptation embedded in this view of martyrdom? T. S. Eliot thought so.

In the early 1920s Eliot struck most observers as an unlikely individual to wrestle with the meaning of Christian martyrdom. As a young expatriate

American poet he had begun to forge a reputation in the world of letters, most notably with the publication in 1917 of a volume of poetry that contained "The Love Song of J. Alfred Prufrock". This poem, with its protagonist's confession that "I have measured out my life with coffee spoons", captures the irony and futility of modern existence. It was Eliot's masterpiece of 1922, "The Waste Land", that catapulted him to fame. Eliot's poem, with its imagery of death, sterility and desiccation, supplied the controlling metaphor for a generation of young intellectuals who had passed through the savage horror of World War I to emerge into a world of decay and disillusionment. When Eliot wrote of "dry sterile thunder without rain", these young men and women knew they had found their avatar.

Eliot possessed greater depths than his epigones realized, for "The Waste Land" formed but a way station in a journey that had already by 1922 brought him far beyond the sedate Unitarianism of his youth. If he saw Western man trapped in a dry sterile land, Eliot also longed for the healing rains of God's grace to bring renewed life and fertility to that sere landscape. While the Hemingways and Fitzgeralds flirted with despair and nihilism, Eliot continued his search for transcendent meaning. In 1927 he reached a milestone in his spiritual quest, for in that year he received the sacraments of baptism and confirmation in the Anglican church. With God's help he would, as he wrote in "Ash Wednesday" in 1930, struggle to "redeem the time", to bring flowers to bloom in the barren stretches of the Waste Land.

In entering the Anglican church Eliot committed his life to a higher cause. Many of those intellectuals who had traipsed across the Waste Land with him in the 1920s also found such a cause, but unlike Eliot they discovered their meaning in Marxism and their heaven in the Soviet Union. How far Eliot had diverged from his contemporaries appeared in his play of 1934, *Murder in the Cathedral*. Eliot turned to the past, to the England of the twelfth century, to retell the story of the fatal conflict between King Henry II and Thomas Becket, Archbishop of Canterbury and Chancellor of the realm. In focussing on this event Eliot sought more than to pose the temporal against the eternal; what intrigued him most was Becket's martyrdom at the hands of four of Henry's knights.

When the play opens, Becket has just returned to England from an absence of seven years on the Continent where, according to his enemies, he has conspired with the French king and the Pope to overthrow King Henry. Becket, the "tradesman's son" and "backstairs brat who was born in Cheapside", had once been the King's boon companion and as Chancellor, the executor of the royal will. As

Archbishop of Canterbury he has resisted Henry's efforts to make the Church subservient to the state. Becket returns now to his English flock, certain that he faces imminent death, a death he does not fear, for it means blessed martyrdom for God's cause.

Before Becket can fulfill his chosen destiny he must face four Tempters. The first Tempter reminds Becket of the riotous times of old when Becket and the King had reveled in sensuality. All this can be restored, urges the wheedling visitor; besides, "The easy man lives to eat the best dinners." Becket dismisses him scornfully: "You come twenty years too late." The second Tempter plays on Becket's memory of the power he had once wielded, a might that could again be used to bring order and stability out of the chaos that men make of their world. But Becket has seen a higher order:

> Those who put their faith in worldly order
> Not controlled by the order of God,
> In confident ignorance, but arrest disorder,
> Make it fast, breed fatal disease,
> Degrade what they exalt.

The third Tempter tries to convince Becket to league with the barons against an oppressive king. This oily appeal disgusts the Archbishop: "Shall I who ruled like an eagle over doves / Now take the shape of a wolf among wolves?"

Becket turns from these temptations confident that he has successfully resisted their blandishments, when a fourth, and unexpected, Tempter startles him. Here temptation reveals its most insidious form, for this Tempter encourages Becket to rush on to a martyr's grave. You will triumph over Henry, dwell forever in the presence of God and see your enemies in hell, he tells Becket. This shocks the Archbishop; he suddenly realizes that his pridefulness has been driving him toward the glory of a martyr's death. "The last temptation is the greatest treason / To do the right deed for the wrong reason." In his self-scrutinizing agony Becket perceives a supreme truth: God chooses his own martyrs; man cannot decide who shall die for God's glory. Man's pridefulness, ambition and taste for heroics disqualify him from such a momentous decision. As Becket tells his congregation in his sermon on Christmas morning: "A martyrdom is never the design of man; for the true martyr is he who has become the instrument of God, who has lost his will in the will of God, not lost it but found it, for he has found freedom in submission to God."

Becket finally enters that realm of truth and freedom that few attain. He submits his stubborn

will to the divine will; now, at last, he is fit to be a
martyr. Henry's knights arrive; Becket's priests
plead with him to bar the door, to hide, to flee.
Becket tells them quietly:

> Go to vespers, remember me at your prayers.
> They shall find the shepherd here; the flock shall
>   be spared.
> I have had a tremor of bliss, a wink of heaven, a
>   whisper,
> And I would no longer be denied; all things
> Proceed to a joyful consummation.

Henry's knights slay Thomas Becket before the
high altar of Canterbury Cathedral. An archbishop
dies, but the Church gains a saint. Is this not
simplicity itself?

XXIII

KARL BARTH'S

Deliverance to the Captives

No other people in the history of mankind have been so preoccupied as Americans with the theory and practice of freedom. The concept of freedom lies at the heart of the American experience. Do Americans really know what the word means? After centuries of praising, analyzing and savoring freedom have we fathomed its meaning at the deepest levels? For many Americans liberty has degenerated into the solipsistic pursuit of self-gratification. It justifies the aborting of the unborn, allows pornographers to hawk their wares openly and prompts the young and not-so-young alike to cast off sexual restraint. Countless Americans exercise their freedom mainly in the pursuit of money. Liberty has become license and not even a Solzhenitsyn can shock us into an awareness of how we have abused our freedom in the name of hedonism and materialism.

Is life on this earth more than an end in itself? Many Americans—perhaps most—would answer

Yes. If there is indeed more than this world, then we need to push deeper into the concept of freedom, to go beyond democratic elections, constitutional rights, free-enterprise economics and individual self-expression; we need, in short, to enter the realm of the spirit, the only thing that counts ultimately. What does freedom mean here? Christ said that he came to this earth "to preach deliverance to the captives". Karl Barth, the pre-eminent Protestant theologian of the twentieth century, took these words as the theme for a series of sermons he preached in the 1950s in a prison in Basel, Switzerland. Out of this seemingly minor event—a preacher bringing God's word to a group of convicts—came *Deliverance to the Captives*, a book that probes the meaning of freedom and bondage on a level that many Americans—despite their obsession with their liberties—seldom reach.

Karl Barth chose a strange congregation to preach to on spiritual freedom. To these men freedom probably meant only this: to be liberated from the impregnable walls and steel bars that immured them from the world outside, to be free to resume normal lives, lives which in their case had led them to this sorry pass. Their understanding of freedom lay rooted in the perversities of the sinful heart. Barth no doubt recognized the difficulty he faced, but he knew something else as well: these men understood the meaning of captivity;

the walls and bars of their prison kept their bondage at the center of their lives in a way that physically free men cannot understand.

Barth might have let his auditors off easily by exonerating them of culpability for their criminal acts. He could have told them that poverty or broken homes or inadequate education had doomed them—through no fault of their own—to lives of crime. They might have been comforted to know that a cruel and hypocritical society had made them scapegoats for its own wrongs. One might have expected such a message from Barth, for one has grown accustomed to the preachers, psychologists and sociologists who today direct such words to the men and women in our prisons. Barth offered no such cheap consolation. He knew that the ravages of sin had led these men to murder, to steal and to destroy; they had violated the laws that enable sin-cursed men to live together without turning society into a jungle where fang and claw determine the survival of the fittest.

Not only did Barth forgo the easy satisfactions to be gained from pleasing one's audience, but he portrayed to these convicts and sinners the full extent of their—and all men's—bondage:

Believe me, there is a captivity much worse than the captivity in this house. There are walls much thicker and doors much heavier than those closed upon you. All of us, the people without and you within, are prisoners of our own obstinacy, of our many greeds, of our various anxieties, of our mistrust and in the last analysis of our unbelief.

Sin imprisons us, locks us into a cell from whose invisible bars we cannot escape, no matter how "free" may be the circumstances of our lives or the land in which we live. Our physical freedom deludes us, hides from us the full extent of our captivity. Karl Barth's listeners at least had an inkling of what ultimate captivity—the bondage of the spirit—means.

Is there no escape then? Do we live in a Sartrean world with "No Exit", an existence in which nothing can strike off our shackles? There is one way out: Christ came to bring deliverance to the captives, to provide true freedom for all men regardless of their lot in life. Christ became a prisoner, bound over to vindictive judges who sentenced him to die for his crimes. Christ became a criminal that we might be free.

Barth's message comes as no surprise to most Christians. We have all heard it before and perhaps it irritates us to be nagged about something so obvious. Is it obvious? Do we Americans, fortunate to live in the freest land on this planet, need to be reminded of the true meaning of "freedom", that word we bandy about so lightly and capriciously? Do we understand that our captivity may be greater than that of the convicts in Basel? Barth hit the mark when he said: "For man's greatest plight is not to see the light in the broad daylight." We are all captives and we desperately need deliverance.

XXIV

Letters of James Agee to Father Flye

"Come unto me, all ye that labor and are heavy laden, and I will give you rest." James Agee longed to answer this call, but he found no rest in this world. By strictly orthodox standards Agee was a poor Christian—or no Christian at all; his thirty-year correspondence with Father James Flye, an Episcopal priest who taught Agee at St. Andrew's School near Sewanee, Tennessee, records the torments of an anguished—some would say lost—soul. Pascal wrote that he who seeks God has already found him; Agee sought and, to all outward appearances, failed to find, but his letters to Father Flye suggest that God found James Agee. Agee died heavy laden, but what true Christian would define "rest" in purely temporal terms?

To those who knew Agee only superficially he must have appeared a gifted and uniquely blessed individual. Handsome, exuberant, exuding a sense of life's infinite possibilities, Agee swept from triumph to triumph. While still an undergraduate at Harvard he won praise for his poetry from Robert Frost and the critic I. A. Richards; two years after his graduation in 1932 Agee published his first book, a collection of his early verse. In the 1930s he became a successful staff writer for *Fortune*. In 1941 he published *Let Us Now Praise Famous Men*, a report on Alabama sharecroppers that rendered these humble lives with a lyricism and depth of understanding that elevated the book to a category all its own. During the 1940s Agee wrote film criticism for *Time* and *The Nation* and almost singlehandedly raised the reviewing of movies to an art. He made the difficult leap from reviewing to doing in the early 1950s, working on such film scripts as *The African Queen*. Amidst all this he found time to publish a novel in 1951, *The Morning Watch*, a well-received book that promised the emergence of a novelist of note. Two years after his death in 1955 his posthumous novel, *A Death in the Family*, won the Pulitizer Prize. Although Agee lived only forty-five years the external evidence of that short life indicates time spent well and profitably.

How little we know from the public record of a life: James Agee, the acclaimed writer, seldom escaped a spiritual and psychological misery that dogged him throughout his adult years. An impenetrable fog of despair frequently blotted out the joys of his life, and a debilitating psychic depression turned his triumphs to ashes on a cold hearth. Just after his graduation from Harvard he confessed to Father Flye his longing for annihilation through suicide. Agee referred often to his malady: "a dirty and unconquerable vein of melancholy" shot through with "a very deep sense of loneliness". The terrible sadness that lay on Agee's heart appears in a letter of 1939: "I . . . have missed irretrievably all the trains I should have caught."

Though trains might be missed, life at the station had its rewards: Agee's charm and good looks attracted women, and people of both sexes found in him a companion who graced life with his presence. But wives (he had three), children and friendship—even the love and devotion of Father Flye—could not heal the wounds. Too many cigarettes, too much alcohol, too little sleep and the frenetic attempt to invest all his energies in his work exacerbated Agee's troubles. He walked into a trap from which he could not escape.

The Anglicanism of Agee's boyhood brought little solace, but though he left the church, he could not flee from God: he remained one of Flannery O'Connor's "Christ-haunted" Southerners. Agee desperately wanted to believe; he wrote to Father Flye in 1945 "that it seems incredible to me not to be a Christian and a Catholic in the simplest and strictest senses of the words." Doubt pulled him in the opposite direction, leaving him to struggle with a wrenching contradiction; he could not resolve this inner conflict between belief and unbelief: Agee went to his death knowing, as he wrote in one of his last letters to Father Flye, that "much in myself [is] the enemy of all I most owe to God, and most want."

Agee's life ended on this bleak note of spiritual failure, but there is more—a "more" that perhaps can be understood only by those who see the agony inherent in man's search for God. To put it simply: James Agee was an unchurched, doubting sinner; he was also touched with a spirituality—call it even "holiness"—that God sometimes vouchsafes to those who seek and cannot find. In saying this one must take care not to transform Agee into a saint. He must have been a difficult and exasperating person to those who knew him intimately. Two failed marriages indicate the toll that Agee's self-destructiveness took on those who loved him; a man who assuages the pain of existence through alternating bouts of intense work and hard drinking makes life a daily hell for those closest to him. Moreover, Agee's spiritual wrestling often degenerated into self-pitying vacillation. But through the miasma that shrouded his life one glimpses the light radiated by a man of love and compassion, a man who suffered because he saw a world filled with suffering. He held no illusions about his fellow men; his recognition of the evil in man occasionally drove him to the brink of misanthropy. But then a "love and pity and joy that nearly floors you" would sweep over him, bringing with them an emotion so compelling that Agee once told Father Flye that he would die for his fellow men if his death could heal their spiritual sickness.

James Agee doubted, sinned greatly and, through the life he lived, destroyed himself, but he longed for the self-sacrifice and purity of soul of a saint. This longing lifted him to a pinnacle of insight, but it also lay at the heart of his agony. He discerned something that most Christians would prefer to ignore: "The full literal Christian idea . . . would destroy the structure of the world as it is, in proportion to how generally and how uncompromisedly it was followed. . . . [It] is *utterly* destructive to *any* contentment with the 'things of the world' as they stand. . . ." Caught between unbelief and a belief that demanded more than he could give, Agee fell victim to his own spiritual honesty and clarity of insight. Despite the sorry record of his life Agee may well have been more of a Christian than narrow definitions of the faith would admit. At the very least, one can acknowledge that God grants an extra measure of mercy to the James Agees of this world—at least I hope he does.

XXV

WILLA CATHER'S

Death Comes for the Archbishop

The twentieth century has witnessed the proliferation of an oftentimes debilitating strain of thought among theologians and philosophers: an obsession with man's despair as the *sine qua non* of his search for God. In the eyes of some thinkers, to profess comfort and joy in the faith exposes one's shallowness; the road to God goes only one way: straight through the heart of the abyss. The assurance and uncomplicated promises of the New Testament will not suffice; one needs Pascal and Kierkegaard and Dostoyevsky to illuminate the dolorous path of anguish and anxiety. Plunge into the abyss and find God is the only counsel many offer.

This conception of the Christian's plight contains much truth: despair stalks this world and when it seizes a man he may well comprehend for the first time the frightening tenuousness of human existence. Despair can become the mother of conversion. But there are other roads to God and blessed is he who finds them. Willa Cather's novel of 1927, *Death Comes for the Archbishop*, portrays a man who follows the way of rocklike faith and finds security and assurance in service to his God. From among such people have come the illustrious champions of the Church who have spread the gospel of redemption across the globe; one doubts that an existentialist theologian would make an adequate missionary.

Father Jean Marie Latour (a fictionalization of Jean-Baptiste Lamy) is such a champion. In 1850 he arrives in Santa Fe, New Mexico, to assume the responsibilities of bishop to the Mexicans and Indians who dwell in the vast territory that the United States has recently seized in the war with Mexico. Rome has chosen her man wisely, for Father Latour possesses a steadfastness and strength born of devoutness and certitude. The still young priest of thirty-seven arrives in New Mexico at mid-century; the old Archbishop of eighty-six—his work complete—dies in 1889. The life bracketed by these years encounters trial, ordeal and hardship, but it never flags: such is the stuff from which the Church molds her heroes.

Powerful Mexican priests who, without proper supervision from the distant Bishop of Durango, have slipped into sloth and vice, welcome their new superior with a mixture of disdain and hostility. Rich laymen, for whom the Church offers sensuous delight and a buttress to their wealth and position, challenge Father Latour's reforms. The territory's Protestants thwart the Bishop's work at every turn. Poverty and ignorance curse the lives of the peons who form the bulk of Father Latour's charges. The Indians practice a syncretistic religion that grafts elements of Christianity onto their native beliefs. Vast distances and poor communications exacerbate these problems; Father Latour spends long days and weeks astride his trustworthy mule Angelica in an effort to minister to the far reaches of his diocese. At times the enormity of these difficulties brings a spiritual barrenness upon Father Latour that parches his soul like the desert that lies beneath the relentless New Mexican sun. His memories of his beloved France, a land gentled by centuries of European civility, gnaw at his resolve. But the steel in his soul—a steel forged by centuries of saints, martyrs and missionaries— refuses to snap. Father Latour transforms his troublesome see into a land alive with a vibrant Catholicism.

The Mexican peons frustrate Father Latour at times, but the depth of their devotion and the unquestioning simplicity of their reverence win his heart. Their veneration of the Virgin Mother and their childlike joy in the tangible evidences of God's goodness teach him the true meaning of holiness. He watches in awe as an old woman—a

victim of life's brutalities—kneels in prayer before
the altar: "It seemed to him that he had never seen
pure goodness shine out of a human countenance
as it did from hers." These people have little, but
they have everything. As Father Joseph Vaillant,
the Archbishop's indefatigable vicar, says:

> The more I work with the Mexicans, the more
> I believe it was people like them our Savior
> bore in mind when he said, *Unless ye become as little
> children*. He was thinking of people who are not
> clever in the things of this world, whose minds
> are not upon gain and worldly advancement.
> These poor Christians are not thrifty like our
> country people at home; they have no veneration
> for property, no sense of material values.

The newly arrived Protestants of New Mexico—
proponents of the gospel of bourgeois vitality and
rugged individualism—view the Mexicans as
impediments to progress and prosperity; to Father
Latour and Father Vaillant the peons are the blessed
of Christ who hear their Savior gladly. Fortunate
are the backward who suffer from culture lag.

Sad to say, most of today's readers of fiction
would probably find all this rather dull. After
all, Father Latour does nothing of world-shaking
importance: he merely labors among Mexicans
and Indians, administers his see, builds a cathedral
in Santa Fe, lives into old age and dies. By the
standards of bestsellerdom this is not hot stuff,

not the sort of subject that propels a book to the top of the lists and wins a lucrative contract with Hollywood. John Gregory Dunne, by contrast, knows how to write a novel about the Church: witness the success of *True Confessions*, with its cast of sleazy laymen and slick ecclesiastical politicians. Andrew Greeley has found the formula as well: strip priests of their aura of sanctity and expose them as worldly creatures who lust after power and sex. Father Latour simply will not do; if only he harbored some dirty little secret that would "humanize" him. Had Willa Cather been farseeing enough she could at least have conjured up a dash of revolutionary discontent among the peons and Indians, with Father Latour playing the part of Third World clerical agitator. Miss Cather missed her chance.

A curious thing, though: Miss Cather published *Death Comes for the Archbishop* over fifty years ago, yet her rendering of Father Latour's love, self-sacrifice, fortitude and faith in service to the Church continues to enthrall readers who shun the current sensations of the literary marketplace. Gerard Manly Hopkins, the English Jesuit and poet, once wrote: "Fame in itself is nothing. The only thing that matters is virtue. Jesus Christ is the only true literary critic." Take heart from this, ye of little faith: John Gregory Dunne and Andrew Greeley haven't a chance. Willa Cather and Father Latour will outlast both of them.

GUIDE TO FURTHER READING

GRAHAM GREENE

Graham Greene's books are readily available; most of them are still in print and any public library should have many of them. In addition to *The Power and the Glory* (Penguin; paperback), Greene's drama of spiritual struggle appears in *A Burnt-Out Case*, *Brighton Rock*, *The End of the Affair* and *The Heart of the Matter*. His latest novel, *Monsignor Quixote*, returns to this theme, but without the spiritual intensity of his best works.

G. K. CHESTERTON

Orthodoxy is available in a paperback edition from Doubleday-Image. Once hooked on Chesterton one should go on to *The Everlasting Man*, *St. Francis of Assisi* and *St. Thomas Aquinas*. Chesterton's *Autobiography* is delightful, as are the *Father Brown Stories*, which recount the doings of a priest-detective. *What's Wrong with the World* offers an excellent introduction to Chesterton's social thought.

GEORGES BERNANOS

Other than *The Diary of a Country Priest* (paperback from both Doubleday and Macmillan), Bernanos' books are hard to find in this country. Look for *The Last Essays*, a volume that shows the workings of a mind possessed of immense moral force.

ROMANO GUARDINI

Regnery–Gateway publishes a paperback edition of *The Lord*. Anything by Guardini is worth reading, but I recommend especially *The End of the Modern World*, a penetrating look at the rootlessness and drift of modern life.

IGNAZIO SILONE

Bread and Wine is available in paperback from New American Library. *The Seed Beneath the Snow* continues the story of Pietro Spina.

CHARLES WILLIAMS

Eerdmans has a paperback edition of *War in Heaven*. If one takes to Williams' peculiar vision then one should by all means read his other novels; try, for example, *Descent into Hell*, in which he sets forth his "doctrine of substituted love". Williams' *The Descent of the Dove: A Short History of the*

Holy Spirit in the Church is a theological work. Humphrey Carpenter's *The Inklings* examines the Oxford circle to which Williams, C. S. Lewis and J. R. R. Tolkien belonged.

EMIL BRUNNER

The Theology of Crisis is out of print and hard to find; the best place to look for it would be in a good university library. Surely this book deserves to be reprinted.

SIGRID UNDSET

Kristin Lavransdatter is available in a three-volume paperback edition from Bantam Books.

JOHN HENRY NEWMAN

I recommend the Norton edition (paperback) of the *Apologia pro Vita Sua*; this volume, part of the Norton Critical Editions Series, contains scholarly essays which enhance one's appreciation of Newman's work.

FRANÇOIS MAURIAC

The Thomas More publishing house has a paperback edition of the *Life of Jesus*. One should also read Mauriac's *Son of Man*, a meditation on Christ. Mauriac was, of course, a novelist of considerable stature; his oftentimes bleak Jansenist sensibility can be observed at work in his novel *Vipers' Tangle*.

WILL D. CAMPBELL

Brother to a Dragonfly is available in paperback from Seabury. Campbell's recent novel, *The Glad River*, explores the interweaving of those ubiquitous Southern themes of religion, kin and race.

DOROTHY DAY

Harper and Row has recently reissued *The Long Loneliness* in a new paperback edition. Miss Day's *Loaves and Fishes* focuses on the Catholic Worker Movement, while *On Pilgrimage* details her activities in the tumultuous 1960s.

THOMAS MERTON

Merton's books are everywhere; some Catholic bookstores devote whole sections to his publications. *The Seven Storey Mountain* is available in paperback from both Harcourt, Brace, Jovanovich and New American Library. I would recommend in addition: *New Seeds of Contemplation*, *Selected*

Poems, *The Waters of Siloe*, *The Sign of Jonas* and *The Silent Life*. I found George Woodcock's *Thomas Merton: Monk and Poet* a helpful introduction to Merton's life and thought.

JOHN WOOLMAN

Citadel Press publishes a paperback edition of the *Journal*. One should also read Woolman's short tract *A Plea for the Poor*.

CHARLES PÉGUY

Péguy's books are scarce, but well worth the search. *God Speaks* is out of print, but Arno has reprinted *Basic Verities: Prose and Poetry*; *Temporal and Eternal* offers a superb sampling of Péguy's thinking. Daniel Halévy's *Péguy and Les Cahiers de la Quinzaine* is essential to an understanding of Péguy.

REINHOLD NIEBUHR

Leaves from the Notebook of a Tamed Cynic is available in paperback from Harper and Row. The many facets of Niebuhr's powerful mind can be seen in *The Irony of American History*, *Moral Man and Immoral Society* and the two-volume *Nature and Destiny of Man*. June Bingham's *The Courage to*

Change: An Introduction to the Life and Thought of Reinhold Niebuhr accomplishes splendidly the purpose set forth in the book's subtitle.

MALCOLM MUGGERIDGE

Both Ballantine and Doubleday have published *Something Beautiful for God* in paperback editions. Muggeridge's two-volume autobiography, *Chronicles of Wasted Time*, is superb; he is at work on the third and concluding volume. I recommend also *Jesus Rediscovered* and *A Third Testament*.

EVELYN WAUGH

Oxford University Press publishes a paperback edition of *Edmund Campion*. Waugh's stature as a novelist grows with the years; accordingly, his novels can be readily obtained from libraries and bookstores. *Brideshead Revisited* became a cultural phenomenon with the recent showing in the United States of the BBC television series based on the book; the series, though excellent, is no substitute for the book.

C. S. LEWIS

Lewis is probably the most widely read serious Christian thinker of the twentieth century; bookstores are filled with his works, and an entire scholarly industry devoted to his writings has sprung up. *Surprised by Joy*, which sometimes gets lost in the welter of his voluminous writings, is available in paperback from Harcourt, Brace, Jovanovich. In case there is anyone in the English-speaking world who has not read at least a half-dozen of Lewis' books, I suggest they turn to *Mere Christianity*, *The Screwtape Letters*, *The Weight of Glory and Other Addresses*, *Chronicles of Narnia* and the science fiction trilogy which includes *Out of the Silent Planet*, *Perelandra* and *That Hideous Strength*.

St. Ignatius Loyola

Harper and Row has a paperback edition of the *Autobiography*. Also valuable is St. Ignatius' *Spiritual Exercises*.

Léon Bloy

It is difficult to understand why no American publisher has seen fit to keep *The Woman Who Was Poor* in print. *Letters to His Fiancée* reveals the deep anguish and profound devoutness of Bloy's spiritual life. *Pilgrim of the Absolute* contains selections from his writings. In *We Have Been Friends Together* and *Adventures in Grace* Raissa Maritain offers vignettes of Bloy, Péguy and many other leading French

Catholic intellectuals of the first decades of the twentieth century.

T. S. Eliot

Murder in the Cathedral is available from Harcourt, Brace, Jovanovich, but everyone ought to own a copy of the same publisher's *Complete Poems and Plays* of Eliot. Eliot's *The Idea of a Christian Society* and *Notes Toward the Definition of Culture* set forth his ideas on religion and society. Eliot has generated an enormous body of scholarship; I have derived much insight from Stephen Spender's *T. S. Eliot* and Russell Kirk's *Eliot and His Age: T. S. Eliot's Moral Imagination in the Twentieth Century*.

Karl Barth

Harper and Row publishes a paperback edition of *Deliverance to the Captives*. For those who wish to delve into Barth's theology I would recommend *The Word of God and the Word of Man*, *Dogmatics in Outline* and *Evangelical Theology: An Introduction*. Eberhard Busch's *Karl Barth: His Life from Letters and Autobiographical Texts* is indispensable.

James Agee

The Letters of James Agee to Father Flye is out of print. One should definitely read *A Death in the Family* and *Let Us Now Praise Famous Men*.

WILLA CATHER

Random House–Vintage has a paperback edition of *Death Comes for the Archbishop*. Anyone interested in good fiction should read *O Pioneers!* and *My Antonia*.